Returned

CALIFORNIA SERIES IN PUBLIC ANTHROPOLOGY

The California Series in Public Anthropology emphasizes the anthropologist's role as an engaged intellectual. It continues anthropology's commitment to being an ethnographic witness, to describing, in human terms, how life is lived beyond the borders of many readers' experiences. But it also adds a commitment, through ethnography, to reframing the terms of public debate—transforming received, accepted understandings of social issues with new insights, new framings.

Series Editor: Robert Borofsky (Hawaii Pacific University)

Contributing Editors: Philippe Bourgois (University of Pennsylvania), Paul Farmer (Partners In Health), Alex Hinton (Rutgers University), Carolyn Nordstrom (University of Notre Dame), and Nancy Scheper-Hughes (UC Berkeley)

University of California Press Editor: Naomi Schneider

Returned

Going and Coming in an Age of Deportation

Deborah A. Boehm

UNIVERSITY OF CALIFORNIA PRESS

University of California Press, one of the most
distinguished university presses in the United States,
enriches lives around the world by advancing scholarship
in the humanities, social sciences, and natural sciences. Its
activities are supported by the UC Press Foundation and
by philanthropic contributions from individuals and
institutions. For more information, visit www.ucpress.edu.

University of California Press
Oakland, California

Library of Congress Cataloging-in-Publication Data

Names: Boehm, Deborah A., author.
Title: Returned : going and coming in an age of
    deportation / Deborah A. Boehm.
Other titles: California series in public anthropology; 39.
Description: Oakland, California : University of
    California Press, [2016] | Series: California series in
    public anthropology; 39 | Includes bibliographical
    references and index.
Identifiers: LCCN 2016003688 | ISBN 9780520287068
    (cloth : alk. paper) | ISBN 9780520287082 (pbk. : alk.
    paper) | ISBN 9780520962217 (ebook)
Subjects: LCSH: Deportation. | Transnationalism. |
    Mexico—Emigration and immigration—Social
    aspects. | Immigrants—United States—Social
    conditions. | Immigrant families—United States. |
    Illegal aliens—United States.
Classification: LCC K3277 .B64 2016 | DDC
    305.868/72073—dc23
LC record available at http://lccn.loc.gov/2016003688

25 24 23 22 21 20 19 18 17 16
10 9 8 7 6 5 4 3 2 1

Por los que regresan

Contents

Chaos

Artemio described his deportation as a night filled with uncertainty and fear. Several weeks earlier, after having been stopped for a minor traffic violation and driving without a license outside of Dallas, Texas, Artemio, a Mexican national and migrant to the United States, was arrested.[1] He spent two weeks in a county jail, followed by time in a U.S. immigration detention facility where he was told that as an "illegal alien" he was being removed from the country. Then one night while Artemio was sleeping, U.S. Immigration and Customs Enforcement (ICE) agents threw open the door, took him from the cell where he was being detained, and transported him with a group of about fifty other migrants to the border town of Laredo. The busload of Mexican citizens, their wrists and ankles shackled, arrived at the U.S.-Mexico border close to 3:00 A.M. After filing off the bus, the migrants' shackles were removed by ICE officials, and they were pointed in the direction of the bridge that joins the two countries. Artemio, with his fellow citizens, walked into Mexico, expelled from the nation where he had lived and worked for several years.

Among Artemio's most vivid memories of his return are the darkness and the chaos. He described loud voices, disorder, confusion. Earlier, while in detention, other migrants had advised the newcomers to move in a group after their release, warning of the many dangers in border communities. With ICE agents standing behind on the U.S. side of the border, Artemio and the others were met by a large group of people waiting for them, calling out and offering information and services: cab drivers; people suggesting hotels or selling bus tickets; coyotes, or guides, willing to facilitate crossings back into the United States—even that very night. Artemio confided that the experience was terrifying.

. . .

When Artemio was deported, he became one of more than three million others to be formally "removed" from the United States by the government in the past decade. The chaos of that night reflects a broader turmoil that shapes transnational movement today. This book chronicles and tries to make sense of the chaos of the current moment. The early twenty-first century has been characterized by unprecedented numbers of deportations of migrants, in the United States and around the globe. In the name of state sovereignty and national security, nation-states are increasingly carrying out deportations—or what the U.S. Department of Homeland Security (DHS) terms "removals"—of foreign nationals. Restrictive immigration legislation and border enforcement are expanding, and debate about immigration and deportation is at the center of public and policy agendas. This age of deportation is marked by both order and disorder. Through calculated efforts, the U.S. state deports hundreds of thousands of undocumented migrants each year. By expelling those it labels "alien," the state ostensibly aims to create stability. Yet this system of supposed order also depends on and results in—and may even intentionally create—disorder for millions of formal and informal residents of the nation.

I pay particular attention to the alienation and chaos of deportation in family life, tracing the contradictory ways that state policies unfold within families and communities. Deportation and other resulting forms of return are disorienting, extending and intensifying the separation caused by migration:[2] families are divided and reconfigured, parents and children live in different nations, partners do their best to maintain relationships that span international borders. The effects of deportation reach far beyond the individual deportee, as family members with diverse U.S. immigration statuses, including U.S. citizenship and residency, return after deportation or migrate for the first time. Families in Mexico are also affected; for example, when Artemio was deported, vulnerability came to define his daily life but also that of his wife and young children, those who depended on his earnings from work in the United States. The state's removal of some is experienced within families by all, as the dis/order of the state reaches into kin networks and strains and reconfigures family relations.

A parallel and intertwined line of inquiry situates this chaos in structural context. There is an order to the mass deportations that the United States has carried out in recent years. A focus on the disorienting effects of deportation reveals the calculated strategies of "the state" in its many forms. This order both contrasts and informs the chaos of deportation. By detailing the experiential and embodied realities of individuals and families, I also uncover the cumulative effect of state action, a product of the diverse actors, including governing bodies, policy makers, and representatives of government agencies, who design, formulate, implement, and reimagine U.S. immigration and deportation laws. Ethnographic research shows the ways that exchanges between state agents and migrants—whether legal and judicial or informal and undocumented—shape this structured chaos. As the stories of those who have been deported make clear, millions of people have not been expelled from the United States by chance.

This book provides a new framework for understanding return and deportation: state actions intended to bring order to the nation and its borders result in its inverse, creating chaos for those who are deported and their loved ones but also for the state itself. Through removals, the state erases presence, undermines well-being, disrupts migration flows, unravels families across borders, upsets life trajectories, and undoes diverse forms of national membership. Today millions of de facto citizens—those who have come and settled during decades of formal and informal recruitment of migrant labor—live in the United States without rights. Furthermore, U.S. citizens, the family members of those who are deported, are also swept up in the devastation of deportation. By removing de facto citizens and, through family ties, U.S. citizens, the state erodes the very notion of citizenship it aims to protect, creating and perpetuating chaos within and beyond the nation.

This book, then, aims to record chaos and structure in its many forms and to theorize the structured chaos of return. It follows movement between two specific nations and in a particular historical moment, but it is also a broader study of return and deportation, processes that are increasingly being carried out by nation-states in many parts of the world. Although I focus on events and exchanges on the ground, the book captures changes that are much larger than any one individual's experiences or a particular nation's system of membership. In the end, this is a study of an emergent global order of social injustice and its

formal statement [margin annotation]

local and transnational effects. As Artemio was removed from the nation, he was emblematic of the disorder, confusion, unpredictability, and violence that characterize the record numbers of deportations being carried out each day in multiple local settings.

As places of departure and destination blur, migrants, deportees, and other transnational subjects describe "going" and "coming" in ways that challenge traditionally linear understandings of migration. By considering the experiences of those who have been deported and their loved ones, I explore this global shift in human experience. In the following chapters, there are accounts of precarity—struggle, suffering, and loss—but also of resilience, flexibility, and imaginings of what may come. This is a world inverted, where certain acts are quickly and often arbitrarily labeled crimes, while crimes against personhood and humanity go unwitnessed and unacknowledged. As deportations are enacted around the globe, it is imperative to understand the character, reach, and effects of return in its many forms. This book tells the story of the chaos, and design, of deportation and its aftermath.

CHAPTER I

Destinations

Your government is throwing everyone out!

—Raúl

"You've heard, haven't you, about *los deportados* [the deportees]? There are many who have returned. It seems you are sending us all back!" Mariela was tidying the house as we spoke. She walked into the courtyard, threw some food to the dogs there, and came back inside. Her joking tone quickly passed: "*Quién sabe que van a hacer* . . . *¿Quién sabe?* [Who knows what they are going to do . . . Who knows?]." When I first went to rural Mexico to conduct fieldwork in 2001, everyone in the community was talking about migration north—a family member who was there, plans for one's own migration, life on the other side. Years later, the conversation had shifted notably. Now as people welcomed me into their homes and chatted with me at community gatherings, they had a common topic on their minds: return to Mexico and the experiences of deportees who had arrived in recent months. As Mariela said, the future of those who had been deported and their loved ones was indeed uncertain.[1]

Beginning with my first conversations with migrants—during research about the ways that migration affects family life—transnational Mexicans have repeatedly expressed a desire to "go and come," to move freely between the two countries.[2] This has been more or less a possibility at different points in history, as demonstrated by generations of Mexican migration to and from the United States, but movement has always been in some way defined, controlled, facilitated, and/or prevented by the state. As a result, the mobility and immobility of people between Mexico and the United States over time has directly served the state. Even when movement has been relatively open, the terms have been set by the U.S. government.

What does it mean to return in the context of deportation? How can we understand departures and destinations in this disorienting milieu? Deportation touches many lives and includes multiple forms of return: being returned, returning, "returning" for the first time. The return of deportation can be removal, forced migration, return migration, exile, displacement, or homecoming. Although states enact deportations as supposed returns, the very notion of "return" is problematic.[3] Is return a revocation? A regression? A reinvention? As I demonstrate, deportation by the state reverses, or undoes, several processes. Removals, and the multiple forms of return that follow, upset the geographic direction of transnational migrations, confuse temporal narratives, strip communities of a sense of security and well-being, deunify families, separate couples, disorient young people, and problematize—and in the end, erode—citizenship and de facto membership in the nation. The difficulty of assessing removal's multiple effects rests in large part on the disappearance of its subjects from the geographic and social scene, its official emphasis on unidirectionality, and the overwhelming right and power of the state and its apparatuses. Yet removal's dis/order and dismantling can be traced through returns, as people go to and come from nations north and south.

RETURNED

The many forms of transnational movement I describe throughout this book begin with deportation, expulsion, or "removal." This is return by force—the act of being returned—carried out at the borders of the nation and from places within the country's interior. Since the 1990s, deportations of foreign nationals from the United States have been on the rise.[4] Mexican nationals make up the largest number of individuals identified by DHS as "deportable aliens," foreign citizens who may be deported.[5] The statistics tell a story of increasing removals, with record highs, for example, of 478,000 foreign nationals detained in 2012[6] and more than 438,000 people removed in 2013.[7] Removals—forced returns carried out by the state—are ever more common, in the United States and elsewhere.

As a result, the number of deportees and other returnees living in Mexico grows as people arrive each day. The many statistics on deportation reflect the experiences that I witnessed during research. In 2001, when I first went to a Mexican farming community with approximately three hundred inhabitants, I heard people talk about only a few cases of deportation in the area, but I knew no one personally who had been deported. In 2008, six people had been returned. In 2010, nearly twenty community members had been deported from the United States, and in 2011, as a year of fieldwork came to a close, more people continued to arrive after long stretches in *el norte*. The numbers of family members who have returned with or followed deported loved ones, as well as those who have come back because of the increased risk of deportation in the United States, are much higher than those the government categorizes as "officially" removed, changing the character of communities throughout Mexico.

As the number of removals grows, so do the legal consequences. DHS distinguishes between "removal" and "return": removal is what is commonly understood as deportation, a legal process with "administrative or criminal consequences placed on subsequent reentry owing to the fact of removal";[8] return is "not based on an order of removal."[9] According to DHS, the majority of "voluntary returns" are those of Mexican nationals who are apprehended by U.S. Border Patrol agents and then sent back to Mexico.[10] Notably, these supposedly voluntary returns have declined, while removals, or formal deportations, have reached a record high.[11] In other words, "returns" as they are officially defined are decreasing, while deportations or "removals"—with their accompanying legal ramifications—are ever more common.

Current deportations of Mexican nationals must be considered "within a long historical frame"[12] of migration between Mexico and the United States. Previous "returns" to Mexico have frequently been forced, for example, the "repatriation" of Mexican (and U.S.) nationals after World War I (1920–23), during the Great Depression (1930s), and through Operation Wetback beginning in 1954.[13] In addition, many other forms of return have been understood as "voluntary," such as seasonal migration, although, as is evident through the returns of removal, this forced/voluntary dichotomy inadequately captures the many complexities of transnational movement over time.

For Mexican nationals, and for those with ancestral ties to Mexico, the U.S. government's systemic removal of people living within its borders is both reminiscent of and a departure from mass deportations of previous eras. Although return and involuntary removal are familiar processes for Mexicans, since the mid-1990s return migration to

Mexico has taken on a shifting character. According to oral histories I conducted, migration and return were relatively open from the late 1970s through the early 1990s. In fact, many migrants received amnesty under the Special Agricultural Worker provisions (SAW I and II) of the Immigration Reform and Control Act (IRCA) of 1986. However, the U.S. Illegal Immigration Reform and Immigrant Responsibility Act (1996)—which systematically criminalized undocumented migration— and the government's response to the events of September 11, 2001, have set the stage for the current increased control of undocumented migration through deportation.[14]

LOS QUE REGRESAN

When Mariela described the many people being "sent back," she listed first those who were returned by the U.S. government. But as she talked more about the uncertainty in people's lives, she also described the networks of family members affected by removal and the many other forms of return that accompany deportation. She spoke of the young children of one deportee and concerns surrounding their father's ability to provide for them now that he had been expelled from the United States. She told me about a man whose teenage daughter had just arrived in their small town, against her wishes, more than a year after her father's deportation. Mariela captured the uncertainty for those who are returned but also for those who return, who come to Mexico for the first time, or, because of age, gender, or other aspects of subjectivity, who may never migrate to the United States but depend on the migration of others. Deportation alters many lives, even those of individuals who have never gone north.

KEY ARGUMENT

In 2008, the state government of Zacatecas began a program called *Por los que regresan*/For Those Who Return. The program provided grants to aid migrants returning from the United States. The funds were directed to small development projects that would benefit return migrants and their local communities; for example, grants could be used to start a business or to make improvements on a home that a family returned to after a long period away. When I spoke with program administrators, I noticed the fluidity of the broad category "those who return." The program, according to staff, was to provide assistance to any resident of the state who had previously lived outside of Mexico, including return migrants, deportees, or those who had lost jobs in the United States and come back to Mexico looking for work. By grouping returnees with different motivations and experiences, the state government seemed to recognize the diverse meanings of return for its residents and the difficulty of delineating specific categories.

Indeed, migrants and those connected to them experience the return of deportation in many ways: this includes being returned—return *as* deportation—and returning—return *because of* deportation. Artemio was returned, removed from the United States by force. This is deportation as expulsion by the state. As "immigration and criminal law converge,"[15] deportation can take on diverse forms. In this age of "crimmigration,"[16] types of removals are expanding: expedited removal (which bypasses the legal proceedings typically associated with deportation) or removal through judicial processes, deportation from the country's interior or at the border, deportation after or without detention, returns labeled "voluntary" by DHS,[17] removals of individuals, mass deportations through programs such as Operation Streamline, and so on.

Alongside those who are returned are the many transnational Mexicans who also return or who migrate across the international boundary for the first time. These returns are more difficult to track, as they are not easily or generally accounted for in statistics. There are those who return because of the deportation of another, such as Mexican citizens who go back to their nation of origin when a loved one is forced to do so. In addition, there are other Mexican citizens who return after the deportation of a family member, though because they first migrated at a young age, they may have no memory of or little connection to Mexico as their homeland. In this case, "return" is an especially problematic and paradoxical label. In addition, many of those who are affected are U.S. citizens, confounding popular understandings of deportation as a process that expels only persons who are not formally recognized members of the nation. After deportation, the U.S. citizen children and partners of deportees frequently move south. And there are U.S. citizen children—usually very young—who are sent by their parents to live in Mexico because their parents are undocumented in the United States and fear their own deportation. Thus many U.S. citizens who accompany deportees to Mexico have never been to Mexico, placing them in the curious position of "returning" for the first time.

"Deportability," or the threat of deportation,[18] also produces migrations south as individuals and families return because of a pervasive climate of fear among unauthorized migrants in the United States. This kind of preemptive return has been tagged with the politically charged label "self-deportation." As many former migrants told me, "*Ya no vale la pena*"—with fewer jobs and increased risk of incarceration and deportation in communities throughout the country, it may be "no longer worth the effort" to stay in the United States. And finally, there are forms of return that while not caused by deportation, are nonetheless part of the broader context of an increasingly commonplace "going" and "coming" of north-south movement. Such returnees might include a retiree—a previous bracero and U.S. permanent resident—who plans to spend his retirement in Mexico; a labor migrant who returns because an economic crisis makes work scarce; an elder in the community who dreams of returning "home"; or even the bodies of Mexican nationals who have requested that they be "returned" to Mexico after death.

Just as deportation moves widely through families and communities, so, too, does my research. I focus on the multiple forms of return that deportation produces, from the forced expulsion of deportation itself to the supposedly "voluntary" north-south migrations and de facto deportations of U.S. citizens[19] that are driven by the U.S. government's removal of people living within its borders. My analysis focuses on those who are deported and the many people who experience deportation even if it is not technically their own—partners, children, siblings, and parents of deportees—as well as members of communities to which returnees go or come. The reach of deportation is so extensive that it is impractical and unfruitful, if not impossible, to consider deportees in isolation. The fallout of deportation is profoundly damaging. It upends families, unnerves people without formal status in the United States, and frightens those who have ties to undocumented migrants. I consider these many diverse experiences as I piece together the story of return.

Throughout the book, I draw on the lived experiences of interlocutors to demonstrate how people go and come through force or will, move and stay, migrate to some locations or find themselves unable to relocate to others. As their experiences show, tracking emergent processes and experiences of return enables us to begin to document the larger impacts of deportation and its intended and unintended, official and unofficial consequences and effects. I consider the multiple ways movement takes place or is channeled, forced, controlled, or prevented by the state. The very categories or terms for return and those who return—deportees, migrants, returnees—are shifting and not easily assigned. The return and movement of transnational Mexicans is disorienting, as people describe "here" and "there" as unfixed places.[20] These forms of movement can be arrivals as well as departures,[21] passages to multiple destinations, or border crossings in both directions. Narratives of "going" and "coming" capture the chaos and uncertainty of return. Tracing such narratives and the trajectories they describe are a way to follow those forced to leave a nation, and the many others who leave with them.

UNCERTAIN RETURNS

The accounts of deportees and those close to them do indeed focus on uncertainty. Mariela's question, "*¿Quién sabe?,*" was echoed in nearly every conversation I had with interlocutors about return. On the one hand, Mariela's words indicate the unpredictability of migrant experience and the economic and social precariousness of undocumented migrants: anyone might be targeted for removal, and all may be affected in some way by the experience of deportation. On the other hand, her repeated phrase is almost an ironic evocation of the certainty of the trajectories of those who are targeted for removal. Exceptions are rarely made within the current legal system, and so the paths before and after removal are, sadly, common to many. Uncertainties of time, geography, and immigration status thus permeate processes of removal that are themselves conceived of in terms of ineluctability, certainty, and unidirectionality.

This erasure of presence has effects elsewhere and close to home, wherever "home" might be located. Constructions of "illegality" and "deportability" in one nation-state can perhaps best be understood by extending an analysis of deportation to migrants' nations of origin or current nations of residence.[22] Legal categories formulated in the United States circulate transnationally. Ethnography among deportees is especially fruitful in explicating processes that may be difficult for researchers to "reach," including "vast institutional machinery—consisting of local jails, prisons, detention centers, INS and FBI surveillance and interrogation, transport, and more."[23] Because the impact of U.S. immigration policy extends well beyond the boundaries of the nation—and beyond any one individual—a primary objective of the book is to examine its effects in multiple contexts and in the lives of the many people touched by deportation.

As ethnographic research makes clear, the chaos of removal is felt (perhaps most) tangibly within family life. Deportation unravels kin networks. State regimes permeate family relations and re/structure kinship, underscoring the ways that relatedness and family dis/connections shift and endure within processes of return. While there is a well-developed body of work about how kinship is structured as a result of migration,[24] how families respond to deportation and return migration is much less studied,[25] largely because these are processes in the making. As the state upends family life through deportation, the kin relations at the center of this upheaval have been an important focus of my study.

Although deportation is ostensibly targeted at individual subjects, it is an assault on family life and one's embeddedness in kin relations. Here, family and gender relations can become channels of control for the state.[26] Through deportation, the state does not discipline only individuals; it also disciplines the loved ones of deportees, regardless of U.S. immigration status. As with migration, the presence of the U.S. state permeates family life as it carries out deportations. What distinguishes deportation from migration, however, is the intensity, and presumed permanence, of state actions related to removal.

Thus contradictions play out in the everyday lives of those touched by deportation: order and disorder, predictability and unpredictability, permanence and impermanence, structure and chaos. Movement through time, across borders, and through categories of membership is often assumed to be easily delineated or even immutable, be it migration from one country to another or the inheritance of birthright citizenship. In fact, such experiences, particularly when framed by return, are fragmented and disorderly, a series of disruptions. Here I outline the un/certainties of removal across time, space, and status, themes that are extended in subsequent chapters. Throughout the book, I consider the bumpy, uneven ways in which individuals and families affected by removal are situated temporally, geographically, and within and outside of categories of belonging.

Unmaking Presence, Family, Future, and Membership

The experiences of Rodrigo bring into relief ambiguities of place, time, kin, and categories. Rodrigo lives in a binational, mixed-status extended family: his parents and adult siblings are U.S. residents, many of his children are living in the United States as unauthorized migrants, and he has grandchildren who are U.S. citizens. In Mexico, he has siblings, children, and grandchildren. Rodrigo and his family members have experienced many migrations and returns over time. In the 1980s, Rodrigo lived in the United States for an extended period, though he returned to Mexico because of health problems, and therefore he did not receive amnesty through IRCA as several of his family members did. Years later, however, he was able to obtain a tourist visa, which allowed him to visit three generations of family members living in New Mexico. Prior to 2006, Rodrigo and his wife had traveled twice using their visas without difficulties, each time careful to return to Mexico within the six-month period for which they were granted permission to be in the United States. Rodrigo explained to me that he did not want to break any U.S. laws, and so he always had come back to Mexico within the allotted time frame.

On his third trip north, Rodrigo's experience was quite different from previous border crossings. When he arrived at the U.S. port of entry in El Paso, Texas, and presented his passport, he and his wife, Teresa, were taken aside, each questioned for several hours separately because, as outlined in the "Notice to Alien Ordered Removed/Departure Verification" he was given later, Rodrigo was "suspected of being an intended immigrant." Like the everyday lives of undocumented migrants in the United States, this border crossing was filled with fear for both Rodrigo and Teresa. Ironically, he experienced deportability and was deported without actually having entered the borders of the nation and despite legal permission from the U.S. government to do so. His Mexican passport, with the valid U.S. visa inside, was confiscated, and he was formally "removed."

The questioning of Rodrigo by a U.S. Border Patrol agent reveals intersecting scales of time, place, and status. According to Rodrigo, the agent pressured him to discuss years in the past when he had worked without papers in the United States. Curiously, this time during the 1970s and 1980s was the precise period when individuals who received amnesty through IRCA were also working in the country without documents. For example, two of Rodrigo's brothers, now U.S. permanent residents, both worked with Rodrigo, first in agriculture and then for a construction company. The agents also asked about his place of residence during these years and since receiving the visitor visa. When did he first migrate to the United States? How long did he live in Mexico after returning? Where did he stay during previous visits as a tourist?

Here, past, present, and future events, multiple geographic locations, and a range of statuses vis-à-vis the U.S. state converge in unsettling ways. In this moment, this one afternoon, Rodrigo's future trajectory took a certain, seemingly permanent turn, based on events that occurred decades ago. Places, too, blurred, as an intended trip north to the United States underwritten by the authorization of a tourist visa quickly transformed into forced movement south, a transnational traveler's border crossing abruptly stopped and reversed by a sudden shift. At the border, Rodrigo's status changed from a category of relative mobility—that of "nonimmigrant" with a "visitor visa"—to one that would shape any future transnational migration, that of "deportee." The labels "alien" and "illegal immigrant," attached to Rodrigo's unimpeded migration decades before, surfaced in the context of migration and border politics of today. Paradoxically, Rodrigo, like others I spoke with during my research, was deported while following the law. As he described, his commitment to respecting U.S. authority and regulations had motivated his initial application for a visitor visa. Acquiring a visa also involved an uncertain process: it had been expensive, lengthy, and—because of very low rates of tourist visa approval in the region—unlikely, but he and his wife were successful in securing the visas. Now, however, they were barred from legally entering the country in the future.

Just prior to his removal, Rodrigo was given a stack of paperwork, including a transcript of his exchange with U.S. Border Patrol agents. Then he and Teresa walked across the pedestrian bridge at El Paso–Ciudad Juárez and took a cab to the bus station for their eventual return to their small town. Several of the questions in the transcript of Rodrigo's removal documents aim to verify the clarity of the proceedings and his understanding of the events; the transcript ends on a definitive note, with Rodrigo's signature at the bottom of the document indicating that the information was correct and that he understood the ramifications. Now, in the eyes of the law, he was a "deportee."

However, while these documents represent the proceedings as clear and straightforward, they were, for Rodrigo, a source of great confusion. When I spoke with him about the experience, there was little certainty, a rendition of that day quite different from that indicated in the official documents. "I didn't understand it . . . honestly, I'm still not sure what happened. It was all very confusing. My wife was in another room, and so I was worried about her. Also, I was concerned that they would go after my [family members in the United States] and punish them," he said. He showed me the forms and asked if there was anything that could be done. Could I, he wondered, at least explain to him what it all meant? Could he return to the United States sometime in the future or was he permanently banned from entering?

Un/predictability of Place

In the context of removal, places are uncertain and future destinations and locations unknown and unexpected. Deportation removes people from the nation: through geographic displacement, the construction of legal categories, and an intensification of laws and their enforcement, states erase the "presence" of particular human beings. The migrations of return and removal are uneven, characterized by both transnationality and limited, restricted, or even completely prohibited movement. Mobilities can be involuntary, such as deportation itself or the relocations of very young migrants. Such "forced" transnationalism[27] is frequently experienced in ways more parallel to movement as the result of war or exile than labor migration. Far from places they understand to be home and regardless of formal attachments or government recognition of membership, people experience geographic displacement as well as dis/connected ties to identities that transcend place.

Similarly chaotic, and both predictable and not, removal can include immobility, as individuals find themselves trapped within one nation, be it the United States or Mexico, with few possibilities for transnational movement and despite concrete ties to more than one place. Such immobilities repeatedly result in divided families—with one member far from others or families split, with partners, children and parents, and siblings separated by the borders of national territories. These configurations of family intersect with the uncertainties of time; intimate living arrangements thought to be permanent can be suddenly dissolved by deportation, while family members once living apart can unexpectedly find themselves geographically close to kin. As with migration, families are again restructured, this time because of removal, with loved ones situated in unpredictable places.

In the context of removal, there is also un/predictability in the direction of movement. In cases of deportation, people typically move from north to south rather than south to north as with previous notable migration flows from Mexico. Yet removal can also produce new transnational migrations north. Deportation thus is experienced as, accompanied by, and generates many other forms of return. Even those deported may be willing to risk the potential consequences of return passage to the United States, "reentry" after deportation that many understand as their only alternative. The predictability and unpredictability—and permanence and impermanence—of future locations create chaos in the lives of those removed and those who are close to them.

Temporal Un/Certainty

The temporal dimensions of return are nearly always framed by narratives of un/certainty.[28] Both migration and deportation are understood in terms of time and are "temporally complex,"[29] or what the anthropologist Cati Coe has termed "transtemporal."[30] These transnational processes represent a convergence of temporal scales, a collapsing or interdependence of past, present, and future.[31] Migration is clearly linked to the past through the historical factors that have shaped movement. Another connection to the past is the fact that family and community members from different generations have migrated at a previous point in time, whether as braceros in the 1940s or as unauthorized migrants last month. Migration is also in the present, experienced as subsistence for families through remittances. Finally, Mexican migration to the United States is nearly always focused on that which is yet to come: people repeatedly equate migration with their hopes for a secure future, for themselves but especially for their families and children.[32]

Deportation, in contrast, is nearly void of future imaginings, except as expressions of the future as unknown or a definitive dead end. Here, too, past individual experiences collide with present events and future trajectories. Previous actions that seemed insignificant or at least commonplace, such as obtaining a social security card, can have a lasting, calamitous effect. Life in the United States—and the support to Mexican communities provided by labor migrations—is understood as fleeting, since one can be deported at any time, while deportation and the threat of removal are persistent, a perpetual state of unpredictability that frames unauthorized migration and state removals. Attention to temporality shows how uncertain trajectories are, paradoxically, accompanied by a sense of surety, especially as the permanence and immutability of state action.

Temporal un/certainty, then, frames discourses about migration, but especially discussions of deportation and the movement that stems from it, and in particular highlights the many aspects of transnational return that are driven by broader forces or that cannot be controlled. Migrants hope for "*suerte* [luck]" and acknowledge the limits of individual agency: "*Así es la vida* [That's life]." Such tropes are expressions of social reality or what the anthropologist Maria Tapias has termed the "embodiment of social suffering."[33] These statements point to the vast "gulf between who is in and who is out,"[34] a divide created by the expulsion, displacement, and attempted erasure of transnational subjects. Un/certainty of time shuts migrants out of a life once known and destabilizes hopes for the future.

Un/Documented Citizens

The same sorts of rigidity and fluidity at work in the temporalities and locations of deportation permeate the categories that define who is included in and who is excluded from the nation. While all transnational subjects embody ambiguity to some extent, removal and return make such category crossing that much more evident. Central to this question is scholarship about the construction of "il/legality" and "il/legal" subjects.[35] Such research emphasizes the historical, political, and social context in which states define migrants as "legal" or "illegal," "in" or "out" of the national body. Similarly, research on citizenship has complicated the many ways that membership is constructed, granted, and withheld from those who cross national borders.

The categories assigned by the U.S. government are plentiful even as they limit or constrict identities: "deportable," "illegal alien," "criminal alien," "permanent resident," "citizen," "noncitizen," "naturalized citizen," and "guestworker," among others. "Aliens" are further distinguished, such as the categories used by government agencies, including "alien worker," "alien entrepreneur," or, especially relevant to this discussion, "alien relative."[36] Yet even as the U.S. state employs an extensive system of categorization that would seem (to seek) to stabilize those persons and identities it assigns to categories, the categories themselves in practice are much more fluid than not. No one neatly fits in any one legal category created and imposed by the state, hence the proliferation of the categories themselves.

State categorization of authorized/unauthorized or documented/undocumented migrants is not easily delineated as the state enacts removal: deportability results in deportation erratically; many migrants find themselves in legal limbo or "liminal legality";[37] migrants may be deported while aiming to or in fact following the law; U.S. citizens are exiled through de facto deportation; and citizens of both nations experience binational bureaucracies in the spheres of education, property ownership, and social services. "Aliens" can be de facto citizens, and U.S. citizens can be easily converted into "aliens." Seemingly static statuses change through legal processes, with membership made available through naturalization or formal citizenship made impossible after deportation due to a felony conviction.

Similarly, there are chaotic elements to the labels by which migrants are perceived by themselves and by others, including academics: returnees, deportees, de facto deportees, migrants, unauthorized migrants, undocumented migrants, undocumented migrants, citizens, contingent citizens, undocumented citizens, de facto citizens, expatriates, refugees, and exiles, among others, make up those touched by removal. These labels also shift through various exchanges and resituatings, and, not surprisingly, lived experience may be altogether different from the seemingly distinctive categories of transnational movement. For example, a teenager who is deported after living in the United States since infancy shares much with U.S. expatriates or even exiled citizens because a return to one's "home" nation could result in arrest and imprisonment. A deportee who is removed while crossing the border for the first time or after a brief stay in the United States is perhaps best understood as a migrant, since both migration and return happened in short succession. Of course, one notable difference after formal removal by the state—rather than return as part of circular migration—is that the legal stakes are high and indeed increase if the individual "returns" to the United States after deportation. Thus I present this research with recognition of the complexities inherent in labeling but also as a way to interrogate, problematize, counter, or reframe the politics of categorization.

Labels, categories, and systems of classification, then, are both multiple and limiting. That one is categorized is inevitable, and how one is categorized has very real and lasting effects, but the metrics and definitional complexity of many categories reveal a less certain and less stable system. In the end, state removals undo or erode citizenship and belonging more generally. Of course, removal itself aims to formalize exclusion, as people are expelled from the nation and assigned a status that legally marks individuals as outsiders or foreigners. Another consequence of the current increase in removals, however, is the way that deportation actually undermines citizenship in its many forms, including state-recognized citizenship, the very membership against which those who are expelled are defined. This is the conundrum the state faces as it attempts to clearly delineate lines of belonging and exclusion in an environment where such an endeavor is ever more difficult, if not impossible.

What is striking about the current wave of deportations is how citizenship, as it is denied for some, is eroded more generally as a system of classification. Membership—as de facto, undocumented, or cultural citizenship—is certainly negated for the deportee but for many others as well. By focusing on the lives of people affected by U.S. immigration policies and the government's removal of migrants from the nation, this is a study of how the nation-state exerts control across time and space, excluding millions from full membership, including its own citizens.

DEPARTURES: AN ETHNOGRAPHY OF RETURN

Mexico City's main plaza, the Zócalo, contains layers of history. A central site of power for the multiple regimes that have ruled what is now Mexico, the area includes structures that have been built and used for centuries—by communities before Spanish conquest, by rulers during the colonial period, by government bodies after Mexican independence, and by contemporary politicians. I had visited this place many times but found myself there again as I embarked on a year of Mexico-based research on deportation and return migration. As I looked at an ongoing excavation of the Templo Mayor, a sacred space for indigenous peoples, a man behind me called out in English. "Hey, hey you . . . can you spare some money?" I turned around, not sure if he was addressing me, since the Zócalo is packed with tourists, many from the United States. He pointed to me and nodded. "I'm in a bad place," he continued. "I used to live in your country—fourteen years in L.A.—but I was just deported. Do you have any cash? I have nowhere to turn. Can't you help me?"

Initially, it seemed quite a coincidence that on my first days in Mexico as I began a new research project on deportation, a stranger, a recent deportee, would approach me. I understood later, however, that it was a fitting exchange to take place during my visit to the center of Mexico's Distrito Federal. Mexican nationals currently make up the largest group of documented and undocumented immigrants living in the United States[38] and the majority of those who are removed by the U.S. government.[39] The deportations of Mexican citizens from the United States are adding a new layer to Mexico's history, but unlike before conquest, under Spanish colonial rule, or post-independence, deportation is not (yet) a site for excavation or readily visible in archives or artifacts. Instead, our conversation pointed to the more ephemeral aspects of deportation. This is a social process that can best be traced and recorded through the words of those who have themselves experienced removal, such as the deportation of this man who, along with millions of others, was cast out of one place and exiled to another.

This ethnography is a new direction in my work that builds on nearly a decade of research in which I have examined the intersection of gender, relatedness, and il/legality among migrant families. It begins where my first book, *Intimate Migrations: Gender, Family, and Illegality among Transnational Mexicans,* left off.[40] As I was completing the research for *Intimate Migrations,* mass deportations had begun, a change that has affected nearly every interaction I have had with migrants in recent years. The book, then, is a continuation of previous research but also, significantly, a departure from it. The experiences of those affected by deportation call for both an extension and reconceptualization of contemporary ways of understanding global movement. Building on my previous work on immigration, I consider the novel aspects of removal and return in the context of transnational movement that preceded this current age of deportation. In its reflection on the past and that which came before, this ethnography is itself a departure that is also a return, as I revisit findings from earlier ethnographic work.

Research in Multiple Destinations

My analysis is based on binational and multisited ethnographic field research among transnational Mexicans with ties to the states of Zacatecas and San Luis Potosí, Mexico, and several locales in the U.S. West, primarily in California, Nevada, New Mexico, Oregon, and Texas. Most research was conducted in people's homes, although I have also worked in sites ranging from federal courtrooms and government offices to spaces such as city parks, street corners, truck beds, and taxicabs. The study is built on fieldwork in multiple places: in rural communities, county seats, and urban centers in north central Mexico and in communities throughout the U.S. West, including Albuquerque, New Mexico; Las Vegas and Reno, Nevada; Tucson, Arizona; and Oregon's Willamette Valley. Because of the frequent movement of those deported and those affected by the deportation of others, this research has also, by necessity, transcended geographic place to include ongoing communication with far-flung research participants by telephone and via email and social media. The sites where I have conducted research are themselves an important part of the story of return, but the relationships among migrants—those severed and those strengthened—are even more significant.

I first began ethnographic research about migration in the 1990s, and have been conducting transnational study focused explicitly on deportation and return since 2008. The project has included binational fieldwork with deportees and their family members, in Mexico in 2008 and as a Fulbright-García Robles Scholar for an academic year during 2010 and in the United States in 2009 and since returning from Mexico in 2011. My findings are based on qualitative research methods, including interviews and life histories; participant observation of, above all, family life but also public settings and community events; visual methodologies such as photography and videography, as both prompt and product of the research; and work with immigrant advocacy and local grassroots organizations.

The ethnography has been particularly informed by longitudinal study and relationships developed over years and across long distances. To study the changes brought on by deportation, I have worked with interlocutors directly and indirectly affected by deportation in both Mexico and the United States: primarily deportees and their family members but also immigrant advocates, government officials, immigration attorneys, and community members. I have conducted research with people of all ages, ranging from community elders to young children, and those who represent vast diversity in terms of life trajectory, gender, family position, employment, nationality, citizenship, and immigration status. For this study, I spoke with hundreds of people about deportation and return, some briefly and others on multiple occasions over a period of years. Several migrants who were deported and their families are at the center of my research, and so I discuss them in detail at various points throughout the book; other interlocutors do not appear as frequently in the upcoming chapters, but they nonetheless made contributions that are central to my analysis.

Although I focus on specific individuals and families, this ethnography, like the many forms of return discussed here, cannot be easily or neatly delineated by time, place, or community. As I write, people are being deported from the United States—on average more than a thousand each day—and life stories are being rewritten. Parents and children are separated from one another, partners are divided, families make plans for reunification, deportees migrate again, and U.S. citizens migrate for the first time. Such chaos calls for a different kind of ethnographic fieldwork, research that, as the anthropologist João Biehl argues, can keep "interrelatedness, precariousness, curiosity, and unfinishedness in focus."[41] For example, while I initially understood my research to be about north-south movement, I soon discovered that such a framework could not adequately capture the complexities of deportation. People move both directions because of removal, and their destinations are multiple and often impermanent. Therefore, I found myself repeatedly tailoring my research strategies to these diverse settings and contexts. In the process, I discovered the very chaos and complexities of removal and return that are now at the center of my analysis.

And, finally, a note about facts and the law. Although "facts" and "the truth" are assumed to be central to legal processes, such details are often blurry and difficult to delineate. Deportation can be a profoundly confusing legal process, as even those trained in immigration law explain. I realized early on in my research just how challenging it would be to record *the facts* of deportation cases. Memories are multiple; they fade and transform. Different family members present different perspectives on events; for example, in one case the deportee reported that he had been arrested for a DWI, while a family member said it was because of attempted robbery. Removal is experienced differently by the different individuals affected, and each individual perceives the process and the past in shifting ways. Although it is tempting to focus on events as they are officially documented and to follow the formal record or paper trail of removal, few deportees have such documents or ever received them in the first place. Furthermore, documents can be deceiving, providing partial or incorrect information, as demonstrated by the discrepancies between Rodrigo's account of his deportation and the proceedings depicted in the paperwork he was given. Documents can create alternative or even fictional accounts. And, so, throughout my analysis, I repeatedly return to the words and life events of those affected by deportation. Although this, too, is a partial depiction, it is likely one of the most complete ones we have.

The Direction of the Book

Removal is a reversal in many senses: it upsets well-being and security in nearly every sphere of daily life. Responding to Nathalie Peutz's call for an "anthropology of removal,"[42] I trace narratives of removal and return throughout the book. The words and experiences of migrants provide a particular and telling view of state policies, one that can generate its own return, a revisiting of scholarship that offers new insights about deportation, families across borders, national membership, and transnationalism. By extending analysis to migrants' nation of origin and by uncovering the effects of the formidable U.S. "deportation regime" among families and in everyday lives,[43] this book advances understandings of deportability and its end, deportation.

In a milieu in which one's membership in different nations holds unequal values,[44] expulsion can be devastating. Diverse approaches to removal have directly informed my analysis, including how exclusion and return have been tied to the development of the nation;[45] the racialized character of policing within the United States and at the U.S.-Mexico border;[46] the ways that criminality is constructed and enacted through deportation;[47] and the character of state power as national governments create policies, patrol borders, and implement removals.[48] Through laws, politics, and practices, states alienate, marginalize, and remove human beings from the nation and the collective.

My research also joins scholarship on return migration as im/migrants and/or their descendants "go back" to their or their family's country of origin. However, this literature typically focuses on second or later generations and processes of voluntary return.[49] Research on different forms of first-generation return,[50] including work on refugees and exiles returning to their homelands, has not emphasized forced return migration. The study of deportation as forced return—and all the different forms of return generated by state removals—has particular relevance for scholarship, policy, and, above all, people's everyday lives.

Each of the chapters that follow explores a different aspect of the chaos of deportation. Chapter 2, "Alienation," outlines the processes of criminalization and dehumanization as the U.S. state constructs human beings as "alien." By highlighting the encounters of transnational Mexicans within policed spaces, in detention facilities, and through judicial processes, this chapter considers intentional and arbitrary aspects of the law and dis/order of removal. I introduce several deportees and their kin networks—those I follow throughout the book—to demonstrate how state action produces and results in deportability, detention, deportation, and departures of different sorts.

In chapter 3, "Violation," I develop arguments related to the violence of return and being returned. The past decade has been a period of growing uncertainty for transnational Mexicans, in both Mexico and the United States. Violence in different forms is increasingly the backdrop to—or even the defining character of—the unpredictable aspects of deportation, itself a violent process, such that those who are removed from the nation face risk in multiple contexts. The many stories of fear and terror show how state action in the name of security repeatedly creates insecurity in everyday life.

Chapter 4, "Fragmentation," outlines how deportation and return divide families and re/structure kinship. The deportation of Mexican nationals deeply affects gendered kin relations and results in emergent forms of cross-border and mixed-status families and partnerships. I describe the experiences of migrants who have been deported and their partners and children as a way to further interrogate the gendered and familial disorder of removal and return. A close reading of kinship across time and space reveals the ways that removal reaches into family life, dividing families and disrupting gender relations.

Chapter 5, "Disorientation," explores the everyday lives of young people—both unauthorized migrant children and U.S. citizens—affected by deportation and return. The focus is on children and youth who "return" or are de facto deported to Mexico with deported parents as well as young people who are themselves deported. After deportation, children find themselves out of place, dislocated from familiar settings and disoriented by the chaos of return. Detailing the shared experiences of deported youth and the children of deportees, I reflect on how young people move through spaces of absence and presence in the wake of deportation.

Chapter 6, "Reinventions," explores the narrowing possibilities for those who return. While migration is typically driven by optimism and perceived future opportunities, deportation and return migration often result in despair and limited potential trajectories. In this chapter, I revisit the chaotic effects of deportation as a way to speculate about the future paths of those who return. For those who have been deported and their family members, return requires a reconceptualization of time, place, kin, and self. These are indeed reinventions, even in the most limited circumstances.

Finally, in the book's epilogue, "Lost," I discuss the profound abjectivity of those who are formally and informally expelled from one nation and take refuge in another. The homecomings described throughout the book are multiple and manifold: as migrants and deportees go, come, go and come back again, much is lost, but as the lives of those touched by deportation reveal, return—in its many forms—can guide the nation and those it deports to new destinations.

As I argue throughout the book, by erasing presence, the state undoes residence, home, kin relations, national membership, future trajectories, the safety of communities in both Mexico and the United States, and so much more. And in its efforts to define and stabilize its population in the name of security, ironically, the state undermines the complex, organic relationships that underpin those very categories. Deportations may even translate into disappearances, "spaces of nonexistence,"[51] "phantom lives,"[52] faint outlines of that which came before, and, in the end, profound loss for millions of migrants and their family members.

GHOSTS

"What does it mean to follow a ghost?," Jacques Derrida asks as he traces the injustices of global capital in *Specters of Marx*.[53] Studying unauthorized migration and removal, too, can seem like following ghosts. There are, of course, the dead, those who die as a result of the U.S. government's immigration control and border enforcement. The ghosts of those who passed while attempting passage are always present for those crossing borders and those seeking to understand migration and its effects. But what of those who have been deported and also those who have departed, leaving the United States for a range of reasons associated with the difficulties of undocumented life? These are the casualties of the U.S. state's systematic removal of foreign nationals, even more ghostlike in their often traceless retreat from an analytic lens. As I discuss in the next chapter, presence can quickly convert to absence, as people are forcibly removed from the nation or forced to live in the shadows: here one moment, then suddenly and seemingly gone.

I find myself following ghosts, tracing the outlines of those who are deportable, those who have been deported, and those who have departed "voluntarily" from the United States or been compelled to do so. As the state undoes place, temporalities, family, and membership, deportation is framed by and creates deep loss—of life, of lives not yet lived, of the living. The departures of deportation most often take place as crisis, sometimes visible and sometimes not; the destinations and aftermath of return are much less known. Recording the absence of family, friends, and community members as they move to uncharted destinations is at the center of the book. Doing so is a way to write against processes that "render individuals invisible."[54] The ghosts of those no longer present in the nation call for justice within the chaos and disorder of U.S. immigration and deportation policies. The stories documented here can outline an alternative path for immigration policy, policing reform, and conceiving of the nation. Searching out those who are seemingly absent might guide us to rethink not only policy and its enforcement but also the way we understand belonging and community for ourselves and our neighbors. And so it may be that following ghosts can lead us to a time and place where people "reappear" and the invisibility of individual experience is replaced with a clearer picture of suffering and, in turn, possible solutions.

CHAPTER 2

Alienation

We all fear deportation . . . This fear of leaving the
house—it's annihilating, destructive.

—David

Every weekday at 1:30 p.m. in Tucson, Arizona, seventy migrants appear
in federal court, their wrists cuffed to belly chains and their ankles shackled, physical restraint that is—as one defense attorney said—typically
reserved for only the most dangerous criminals. The image is striking:
rows of primarily young Mexican men wait to be called up in groups of
eight and asked brief questions about their nationality and place of entry
before answering in the affirmative again and again, the repetition of
"*Sí*" only occasionally disrupted by a "*Sí, Señor,*" or a defense attorney
verifying a name change. "Guilty or not guilty?," asks the judge through
an interpreter. On the advice of their attorneys, the defendants have
made a previous plea bargain to a lesser charge, so all respond the same:
"*Culpable, culpable, culpable*/Guilty, guilty, guilty."

Operation Streamline, which began in 2005 under the Bush administration, takes individuals and deports them en masse through an almost
mechanical process. As the proceedings begin, the judge speaks to everyone as a group, explaining the charges and the conditions of the plea
agreements reached that morning. All migrants are charged with the
same infractions: entry and reentry, or, according to 8 U.S. Code 1325
and 8 U.S. Code 1326, "improper entry by alien" and "reentry of
removed aliens." The script of the courtroom proceedings is identical
for all defendants, except for some details such as name, nation of origin, and place where each was detained. Most of the migrants have tried
to cross the border in the last twenty-four to forty-eight hours, picked

up by U.S. Border Patrol agents in the desert near Naco, Douglas, Nogales, Lukeville. With few exceptions, the defendants will serve a sentence ranging from 30 to 180 days and will then be deported.

Watching Operation Streamline, it is easy to see the migrants as a collective of people who have committed the same act and who are experiencing the same fate. Each day, these groups of migrants are alienated quite literally: alienated by their incarceration from any agency or mobility they might possess; constructed as "aliens" and thus as different from and defined against those who are perceived as authentic and deserving members of the nation; removed from any individuality by a mass grouping that treats them all the same. The migrants are collectively shamed, ostracized, othered. As the migrants file out of the room, looking at their feet and surrounded by federal agents, there are few indications of the specifics of their circumstances. In this legal setting, all are alienated in a similar fashion.

Of course, despite the fact that Operation Streamline deports migrants en masse, each individual has a personal, exceptional story that is likely to be quite different from the official record. Here, the speed and supposed efficiency of the process—maintained by means of statistics, lists, rosters, routine—certainly obscure realities. There are some clues to the diversity of everyday lives among the migrants, even in this format that, for the most part, conceals difference. One migrant asks the judge to consider his wife's illness before sentencing him; the judge responds that while he is sorry about the man's struggles, there is nothing he can do. In another case, three family members appear on the same day, parents and their adult daughter. Through their lawyers, they request assignment to the same detention center, in the hope that they will be deported within days of one another and to the same location. A few cases are dismissed, usually when an individual is unable to understand the proceedings because of native language, mental capacity, or educational background.

Although the migrants have many challenges in common—economic hardship, crossing the border through violent spaces, unexpected events along the way, detention by U.S. Border Patrol agents—no story is identical. Each migrant has a home community, somewhere south of the border where family and friends wait. Significantly, most have family members in the United States as well. As one defense attorney explained, 75 to 80 percent of his clients have U.S. citizen children. He said that family ties drive migrants' journeys back to the United States after a previous deportation. "The draw is so strong," he told me. Migrants make the trip despite the weighty penalty of return, if, the attorney added, they are even aware of precisely what the penalty might entail. Each of the individuals in court on any particular day has made a decision to risk personal safety in hopes of gaining security in another form. These are the stories that are rarely known, or ever told, as people are deported each day.

Witnessing these mass deportations, one also witnesses the formal conversion of migrants to "aliens," the legal category used by the state. Yet they are also alienated in a broader sense: through deportation, the U.S. government transforms migrants into foreigners, strangers, others, those who are excluded, or, even—in popular discourse—creatures not from this world. Immigrants are quickly marked "illegal" and "criminal," as well as "alien."[1] This is both "alienation" as estrangement and a kind of "alienization" through which one becomes legally categorized as such.

Here, I consider how deportation, alienation, and dehumanization are entwined. State actions, like their aftermath, are chaotic and contradictory, marked by tensions, confusions, and uncertainties. The process of removal dehumanizes the very human beings the government expels, inexorably and paradoxically creating foreigners in order to deport them. Yet even as rigid categories are constructed and applied, the delineating features of the labels fade. "Illegality," first linked to those formally labeled as "alien," may extend to all family members in mixed-status families. The expulsion of those labeled as "other" thus—even if haphazardly or inadvertently—also banishes the nation's own citizens. Deportation focuses on individuals even as its impact reaches beyond any one person to affect families and communities. These are among the twists and turns of the alienation of the current moment.

DISPLACEMENTS

The alienation of deportation begins with a lessening of the value of certain human beings or, even more chilling, a complete dehumanization. As migrants go through the federal proceedings, they are aggregated into a mass and criminalized. Judges and attorneys underscore that Operation Streamline includes due process, but it is, perhaps, a little less due process than that to which all accused are entitled, or, given the speed with which the proceedings take place—sometimes in less than thirty seconds per migrant—one imagines that due process is not necessarily ensured. In mass deportations as they are enacted in scenes like those in the courtroom in Tucson, it seems that the fix is in: the expulsion of defendants is already determined. Simply stated, the categories—"alien," "deportee," "criminal"—are already (or will inevitably be) assigned.

In a relatively brief period, individuals go from being "deportable" to "deported," "departed," and/or "disappeared." These stages of return are interconnected and overlapping, unpredictable, yet with very real consequences and outcomes. Deportability, even if not determined formally in a courtroom, can also become a kind of de facto detention, as daily life in the United States narrows markedly without documentation. When people are formally detained, they may be released or they may be determined to be "deportable" by the court. Once deportability is determined, the usual outcome is deportation, although even that is not fully determined, as sometimes those deemed deportable are allowed to remain in the United States. Deportation mandates departure, but far more individuals than those who are deported end up departing, vanishing from previous lives and meaningful communities. Finally, many "disappear"—those who are deportable, those who are deported, and those who depart from the nation with others.

One of the common threads that run through these diverse experiences is the *displaceability* of those whose lives are shaped by deportability and deportation. The state easily marks people as "deportable" and, ultimately—to borrow Derrida's term—"displaceable,"[2] justifying and enabling the widespread removals of recent years. An analysis of displaceability shows how people categorized in diverse ways by the state, including de facto and formal citizens of the United States, can be alienated and relegated outside the nation's borders. Because of state policies, those labeled "deportable" and categorized as "displaceable" can be swiftly transformed, summarily becoming those who are deported and displaced. The encounters of transnational Mexicans within policed spaces, with law enforcement officers, in detention facilities, and through judicial processes point to both the arbitrary and the intentional aspects of the law and the dis/order of removal.

For philosophers, *hospitality* can entail welcoming others into one's country.[3] Building on discussions of hospitality and encounters with "strangers" and "foreigners,"[4] I show how the alienation of removal is engendered by profound *inhospitality,* through which a lack of welcome, indeed its complete inversion, leads to expulsion, even when the "visitor" is not so "foreign" or not a "stranger" to the nation in any substantive way. When newcomers, longtime residents, and undocumented citizens of the country (those who are de facto members despite a lack of formal documentation) are removed, expelled, or exiled, they are forced to inhabit irrefutable, if not irrevocable, marginalization. Whether individuals are forced to leave through deportation or compelled to move through undocumented or de facto deportation, the state formalizes the relocation of its members—citizens and de facto citizens—outside the borders of the nation. Through deportation, the nation enacts the alienation of migrants and their loved ones.

The process of making and marking members of the nation as "foreign" or "strange"—this alienation and alienization—is clearly embodied by those migrants who are targeted by state policies. But the effects of displaceability are far-reaching. Through family ties, alienation may be experienced by any family member of a person who is deported. Legal, economic, and affective ties to deportees effectively make their relations potentially displaceable and able to be excluded through state action. My analysis, then, extends previous theorizations of deportability in order to develop the concept of displaceability as a profound form of alienation, one that—because it extends to both documented and undocumented citizens—perhaps goes even deeper than deportability. Displaceability and multiple forms of displacement are produced by U.S. deportation policies. Displaceability crosscuts different statuses assigned by the state and does not attach precisely to legal statuses. Although legal discourse and popular ideology of deportation and "illegality" circulate clearly defined categories, in practice distinctions in the labels are less clearcut, and displaceability is possible for anyone with ties to those who are categorized as "alien" by the state.

Deportable

As we sat at their kitchen table one evening, Fátima and David, migrants living in the United States without state authorization, contemplated deportability, the possibility of deportation. "Life as an undocumented immigrant is uncertain," David told me.[5] "When I go to work, to buy groceries, to pay bills, I am fearful, always fearful. It's dangerous for my family to go out, wondering if *la migra* [ICE] is going to come. We live this way, because deportation would be the end of your world . . . There's no freedom, no emotional freedom . . . People feel closed in, suffocated." David and Fátima have not experienced deportation directly; instead, they are considered by the state to be "deportable." They, like millions of others, live with the profound threat of deportation every day.

personal story

Fátima and David and their three children, Bea, Felipe, and Mateo, first came to the United States on tourist visas. The children were young when the family arrived, and Fátima immediately enrolled them in the local schools. In fact, Fátima said, one of the primary motivations for staying in the United States was the opportunity for an education not possible in their home community in Mexico. They made the decision to overstay their tourist visas to offer their children a better life. And the children excelled in their studies. Bea and Felipe, both honors students, graduated from the state university despite not having documentation. While enrolled as students, they were able to receive state scholarships by signing an affidavit verifying they would "file an application to legalize [their] immigration status as soon as [they were] eligible to do so."[6]

Currently, Fátima and David are living in the country as undocumented migrants. Bea and Felipe are both U.S. permanent residents who changed their statuses when they each married U.S. citizens. Mateo, a high school student, remains without documents. Although no one in the family has been deported, the possibility lives with them everyday. As David described it, those without documents are, in a sense, already detained. He spoke of being "*encerrado*," referencing multiple meanings of the word: enclosed, caught, trapped. Facing the threat of deportation should they be made visible to the state, people are relegated to their homes, excluded from public life, and forced to live on the margins of communities of which they are an integral part but in which, because of their immigration status, they have limited participation.

The number of unauthorized immigrants living in the United States is estimated to be 11.2 million, the majority of whom are from Mexico.[7] The context of deportation, and a story that is much more difficult to tell through such statistical data, includes the everyday lives of Mexican nationals currently in the United States. Indeed, as Nicholas De Genova posits, "there are no hermetically sealed communities of undocumented migrants,"[8] further complicating demographic portraits of unauthorized migration. Undocumented migration, deportability, and removal by the U.S. state must be considered within a frame that recognizes the permeability and shifting character of the supposedly rigid categories that delineate documented and undocumented migrants.

As David and Fátima's experience makes clear, deportability is a constant source of uncertainty for undocumented migrants and those connected to them—including, in their case, their children who are U.S. permanent residents. The fear of deportation can come to define the daily lives of transnational Mexicans living in the United States without

turns into factual reference

papers: "Migrant 'illegality' is lived through a palpable sense of deportability."[9] Even the most quotidian activities—going to work or the grocery store—involve fear and danger, the conscious awareness of possible risk, in the distance and close to home, today or sometime in the future. Those without documents articulate the uncertainty associated with going outside of their homes and support networks. They describe drives across town, meetings at their children's schools, or time on the job as risky, alarming, or perilous. This is the "suffocation" that David describes—this repressive reality that can define daily life for those living without documents.

David, Fátima, and others like them take precautions and yet also go on with life. The bind is clear: while the likelihood of being among those deported is relatively slim, deportation is indeed actualized in communities, and all unauthorized migrants, whether or not they themselves have experienced deportation, have certainly witnessed it—the deportation of a family member, a community member, a friend, a coworker, a parent from their children's school. In a sense, everyone with transnational ties lives with deportability and feels its effects. For example, although David and Fátima's two eldest children have changed their immigration status and have state authorization to be in the country, they constantly face the fear that their parents might be deported. So, while deportation does not effectively reduce undocumented migration, it is very effective at controlling migrants, their families, and broader communities.

In communities throughout the United States, workplace raids, ICE agents serving warrants at people's homes, arrests at the Department of Motor Vehicles or after "routine" traffic stops, and racially motivated violence targeting undocumented migrants have increased, creating a climate that further alienates migrants. For example, in my home community of Reno, Nevada, there have been a series of workplace raids and arrests. ICE agents have carried out raids at places of employment as well as audits of I-9 forms—the forms required by the federal government to verify an employee's eligibility to work in the United States—at several companies. On September 27, 2007, ICE raided eleven McDonald's restaurants in northern Nevada, including franchises in Reno, Sparks, and Fernley, and made up to one hundred arrests, resulting in the detention and eventual deportation of migrant youth—including one young man who had just turned eighteen—and parents with small children.

After President Barack Obama took office and committed to changing the character of immigration raids that had been carried out under

President George W. Bush, the ways that raids were conducted did change to some extent, but their effects did not. Since the raids at several McDonald's locations, ICE has conducted I-9 form audits—presumably in place of raids—at large employers in the area. An audit at a large retail distribution center in 2009 resulted in the release of between fifty and one hundred employees (there were differing reports about the numbers of workers affected), and in 2010 the owner of a local business was indicted for allegedly encouraging undocumented migrants to work at his company.[10] I spoke with former employees of the distribution center shortly after the audits took place. They were told by attorneys hired by the company to advise the migrants—ostensibly about their rights—that personal data would be forwarded to DHS.

These events, whether workplace raids or the supposedly kinder and gentler I-9 audits, have similar impacts: both have resulted in the dismissal, detention, and deportation of hundreds of people and caused countless others to hide or flee. The day after an I-9 audit at a major employer in Nevada, many community members, concerned with their safety and that of their family members, did not leave their homes or allow their children to go out, even for school or work. Some of the migrants, especially those dismissed from positions because of the I-9 audits, felt it necessary to leave their homes to further protect themselves and their families, and so they picked up and relocated to new residences in the area or left the state entirely. Raids and audits—whether or not one is directly affected by them—sow uncertainty and can change future plans in an instant.

· · ·

The tension was thick as families filled the room for an information session about immigrant rights.[11] The meeting, a response to recent raids, had been coordinated by activists and community organizations and featured a panel of attorneys, service providers, and a representative from the Mexican consulate. The attorneys focused on steps to take in the event that a migrant is arrested, preparations in case of detention and possible deportation. Migrants expressed concerns, some specific to their individual cases and others that applied to the collective. As the panelists took questions from the audience, a reality became clear: there is a predictable, if not inevitable, path should undocumented migrants be detained. As the attorneys explained, exceptions are rarely granted, so it was especially important to prevent, if at all possible, arrest and detention.

The meeting showed how lives in the present are repeatedly shaped by preparations to stave off potential risks in the future. Attorneys explained to im/migrants what they could legally do if the police or immigration officials came to their home or work or stopped them in a public place. The organizers handed out booklets explaining immigrant rights and outlined the limited preventive steps immigrants could take now: locate an attorney and always have a phone number on hand, carry an immigrant rights card stating the desire to contact an attorney if taken into custody, make copies of important documents, and—most disturbing to parents—make arrangements for the care of children in the event of an apprehension. But how does one prepare for deportation, a legal process that devastates families, turns lives upside-down, or, as David described, would be the "end of your world"? As the audience well knew, the reach of deportability and displaceability is long. One cannot anticipate the finality of deportation and its limited options: the reality is that most undocumented migrants have no legal recourse and no prospect for alternative trajectories should they be arrested and detained.

In an attempt to reduce the threat of deportation, migrants have responded as they are able, though there are limits to one's countering of the uncertainty of deportability and the displaceability that accompanies it. For example, phone trees, email and text messages, and hushed conversations communicate potential dangers. As Fátima explained, she credits a phone call from a friend for securing her family's safety on one particular day: "A coworker had warned me not to go outside. Her friend worked for *la migra* and tipped her off that raids were to take place that morning. She initially called people she knew, and then we all starting calling and texting everyone we knew. I had my children stay home. We didn't go out. That day, the raids took place." However, Fátima's sense of security was fleeting. "What about the next time?" she asked. "We must be vigilant, the possibility that we will be caught . . . it doesn't end."

This suspension of personal security is a form of alienation and disciplining on the part of the state, "generalized punishment"[12] that monitors individuals, their families, and, by extension, the social body. The doubts and insecurities for deportees and those without papers who could potentially be deported can be traced to the presence of the state in individual lives, through informal and inexplicit modes of control in addition to more specific threats. By fostering a climate of deportability and displaceability, the state produces a shadow of anxious insecurity that follows undocumented migrants. Deportability, as assigned by the state and made tangible in the everyday uncertainty surrounding its inevitability, highlights what the anthropologist Susan Bibler Coutin has termed the "inviability of life."[13] Here, lives are constructed as "expendable,"[14] underscoring the contingency and un/certainty of living lives deemed displaceable and dispensable.

Detained

"It was more or less a prison," said Miguel. "Yes, it was basically prison." Sitting on the steps of a city park in Mexico, Miguel described his border crossing, detention, deportation, and return to his home community—all of which happened in relatively quick succession. But the "prison" he spoke of was not a federal detention center or a county jail, it was small apartment in Houston, Texas. Miguel's harrowing journey started and ended at his home in Zacatecas, a trip that took several weeks but to him seemed much longer. Miguel and a friend headed north, contracting with a coyote who had been recommended by his friend's cousin. The cousin paid an advance deposit for their $1,800 passage and made arrangements for the men to cross near Piedras Negras, Coahuila. The crossing took nearly two days, with the men walking through isolated desert terrain. When they arrived at their destination, they were immediately taken to an apartment and put in a bedroom with a group of twelve other migrants.

So the apartment was the first place where Miguel was detained. Miguel described how he and the others were held hostage for more than two weeks. Miguel and his friend stayed in that room as migrants came and went, waiting while the captors tried to contact the friend's cousin to pay the additional $500 owed for each man's crossing. As one of the smugglers insisted, "You can't leave. We are keeping you here until the money is paid." They told Miguel and his friend that they were in no hurry to release them. "And so for two weeks, I sat in a room as retribution for not paying," Miguel said. The men were treated "very badly." He continued, "We weren't able to leave. The coyotes gave us water but very little food—one day, yes, the next day, no, or two days, yes, and the next day, no. If we needed to go to the bathroom, we had to knock on the door and wait to be accompanied there by the man guarding us." Although the popular perception of a successful border crossing has freedom as its telos, Miguel's experience as the smugglers' prisoner confirms that detention is a very real prospect at all stages of migration.

Miguel was eventually released and taken to Nevada by his friend's cousin, where he began another detention of sorts. Again, Miguel spent weeks confined, in this case in the cousin's apartment: "I wasn't able to go out. The men we were staying with said that *la migra* was patrolling the area and that people were being picked up." And, indeed, the first time Miguel left the apartment, to go two blocks to a convenience store, he was arrested and again detained—this time by U.S. ICE agents. Miguel was shocked: "They started asking questions, and I didn't know what to say. They didn't speak any Spanish. And then they handcuffed me." The officers arrested him and took him to a facility where he was fingerprinted and held for several days.

Miguel had nowhere to turn, no way to get in touch with his friends, no phone number to call, and no one who spoke or understood Spanish well. The agent who booked him was a "gringo" who spoke limited Spanish, but, Miguel explained, "I didn't really understand him either." During the questioning, Miguel became increasingly disoriented. The agent asked if he feared living in Mexico and why he had come to the United States. Miguel was truthful: "I told him that I wanted to earn a little money, to help my family." The agent then asked Miguel if he was, in fact, from Mexico. "He asked if I was from Honduras or another country. He said that I didn't 'look Mexican.' I started laughing, and he said, 'Are you laughing about this? You shouldn't be joking. I'm not joking.' They said I didn't look like I was from Mexico, so I laughed, but I wasn't joking around. They were smiling and laughing, and so I smiled too." When Miguel assured the agent that he was a Mexican citizen, the agent asked him to name the current president of Mexico and to sing the national anthem. With shame, Miguel told me that he was unable to do either well: "I remembered the former president's name, but I wasn't sure about the current one because I don't vote." He sang what he could recall of the anthem but described the agents as mean-spirited and the exchange as confusing and humiliating.

After a few days in immigration detention, Miguel was shackled, put on a bus full of Mexican nationals, driven to San Ysidro, California, and released across the border to Tijuana with no money or possessions except the clothes on his back and a small keychain, of the U.S. flag, in his pocket. "They left us at the bridge," Miguel told me. Then the group went to meet with representatives from the Mexican government. Someone gave him a sandwich and a soft drink, but, Miguel said, the agency did not pay for his bus ticket to Mexico's interior as it does for some deportees. Ironically, Miguel noted, he didn't have the "papers" from his deportation necessary to secure this "benefit" provided to some return-ees by Mexico. When I asked Miguel if he was "deported" or "returned," he said he couldn't be sure "because no one explained it to me." After eating the sandwich, he walked out onto the street and strategized how to get home.

When I asked how he paid for his return trip through Mexico, he became animated. Miguel described the small keychain of the U.S. flag, his only memento from his travels. At a restaurant in Tijuana, he offered to exchange the keychain for food. The owner gave him a taco, and said, "I'm not going to trade the keychain for a taco, I'm going to give it to you." And so, "that is how I got back—I kept offering to trade the keychain for something, a taco or a ride, but each time someone would say, 'No, that's OK, just keep it.'" His trip from the border to Zacatecas took three days. Miguel hitchhiked until he made it home, each time offering to trade the keychain. While he experienced great hardship and alienation in the United States, in Mexico there were many people who extended kindness and generosity to a stranger. And, as an ironic marker of the freedom that seemed ever imminent but failed to arrive, the key-chain remained an important object to Miguel. "I still have that key-chain of the U.S. flag," he told me, smiling.

In Miguel's description of his detention and deportation, there was much uncertainty about the specifics of time, place, and circumstances. Throughout his migration and return, Miguel was trapped in different ways: before departure due to limited options, while held hostage in a room in Houston, during his stay in an apartment in Las Vegas, while detained at a federal detention center, and then as he was released to Mexico with little hope and no viable means of support. As Miguel moved through these different spaces and across time, he experienced alienation in many forms. He was shamed and dehumanized by different actors, from smugglers who held him against his will to agents who ques-tioned the veracity of his identity. Miguel's movement and future were regulated and controlled, while his autonomy was repeatedly compro-mised. Questioning the authenticity of his Mexican citizenship, U.S. agents had even tried to deny Miguel the formal national membership to which he is entitled. In a sense, after his return to Mexico, Miguel was yet again "detained," trapped by a debt that may never be paid in full and unable to adequately provide for his family while working in Mexico.

Miguel's continued entanglement in the debt incurred by his passage underpinned by the lack of economic opportunity in his home commu-nity in Mexico shows both the variety and the length of the alienation and alienization of detention. Returnees describe detention in local jails, transport to and detention in federal immigration facilities, and the process of "removal" as harrowing and shameful. In their accounts of time at a county jail, solitary confinement in federal detention, or "release" while awaiting trial, migrants emphasize the spatial and temporal aspects of removal, the continued sense of un/certainty and im/permanence that accompanies forced return. Migrants speak of being trapped, both when they are arrested and as they imagine limited future trajectories. This is the alienation and alienization of detention, as people are "locked up," literally and in symbolic ways.

While David and others describe being *encerrado*—closed in by the threat of deportation—migrants like Miguel who are detained are *encerrado* in an actual sense, imprisoned by the U.S. government. Although a small minority of migrants are deported without spending time in a detention facility—Rodrigo, for example—most encounter detention in some form, and nearly all are confronted or held by U.S. agents in some capacity. Migrants speak of being "caught"[15] when they are arrested, detained, or given an order of removal. This is one of the most traumatic aspects of deportation for migrants: those who are affected describe detention as a profoundly alienating experience.

. . .

Just before he was deported, while still at a federal detention center, ICE agents brought Jaime the clothes he had been wearing the night he was arrested several months earlier: "They give you your clothes and shoes but not your shoelaces. You can't have anything in your pockets. My shoelaces, cell phone, wallet . . . they put those in a bag with my name on it." After a childhood and life of more than fifteen years in the United States, Jaime had only this small ziplock bag with a few possessions. Three months in a county jail in rural Colorado, followed by several weeks at a federal detention center, had been demoralizing. Arrested just after his eighteenth birthday, Jaime admitted that detention was quite frightening at first, but he soon learned the ropes and kept his head down: "You let people do their thing, and you just do yours." He tried to get used to "the sucky food," and even made some friends. He watched a lot of television, and like Miguel, he waited—first, he appeared in court to hear the charges against him, "then they give you another court date, and then another." So Jaime continued to wait.

Jaime—whom his aunt described as "a good kid who made a mistake"—was forcibly relocated. Jaime migrated as a toddler, and although he was an unauthorized migrant in the United States, his day-to-day life as a teenager was much like that of his U.S. citizen peers: he worked part-time, socialized with friends on the weekends, had a steady girlfriend. But that abruptly changed when Jaime was detained. After Jaime and some friends were stopped by police officers and cited for having open containers of alcohol in their vehicle, their paths went in notably different directions. Jaime's friends, all U.S. citizens, were arrested, quickly released, and ordered by the court to complete community service. In contrast, Jaime's life took a jarring turn.

He spent nearly four months incarcerated. As Jaime was arrested, imprisoned, detained, and deported, he moved through multiple U.S. legal, law enforcement, and immigration systems, all of which alienated him as an outsider to be formally expelled from the nation. His family hired a defense attorney, and he received probation for the initial charge rather than a prison sentence. But then he was transferred to immigration detention, where, the criminal defense attorney told him, he would "need a different attorney." Jaime's father wanted him to have good legal representation, so the family met with an immigration lawyer. But, Jaime reported, "he told me that I didn't have a chance, that he was just going to tell me the truth, that it was going to be a waste of money to pay him. So that's when I decided to represent myself." Jaime's case, like nearly all deportation proceedings, reached an inevitable end.

When Jaime appeared in immigration court to respond to his removal order, he felt it would be best to speak without an interpreter. He told me that he hoped the judge would see how "American" he was and acknowledge the fact that he had been educated in the United States and was, in many ways, from the United States, even if not a formal member of it. Jaime pleaded with the judge in immigration court to consider his ties to the United States but found him "very hard to reach." "People told me that the judge I saw really hates immigrants . . . and I thought, 'that's not what you want.'" As with Operation Streamline, the proceedings went quickly. Jaime appeared with a group of thirty other people, yet no one was given more than two or three minutes. "Everybody watches the proceedings. Each person comes before the judge and then, 'Next.' Almost as soon as you have appeared, they take you back to your room. It's really quick, actually."

When Jaime was deported, agents came into his cell in the middle of the night—as they had with Artemio—and then Jaime, too, faced the chaos of removal. He described a series of dehumanizing scenes, with federal agents in every direction and at every turn. "The agents talk to you like you are not a person. They yell at you: 'Hurry up! Listen! Everybody shut up!' They were very rude, but nobody was talking." Jaime thought it was strange that the agents shouted at them while they were silent and told them to hurry up when they could not do so. As Jaime explained, everyone was cuffed and shackled with a chain between their wrists and ankles, "so you can't really run, you could barely walk."

Jaime's description of detention centered on the dehumanization that accompanies alienization. In prison on the pending open container charge, Jaime could manage his experience by keeping his head down and minding his own business. As he was deported, his individual demeanor and experiences were not acknowledged or considered. In effect, the cessation of being an "American teen" that commenced with the determination of his deportability was completed through deportability actualized: Jaime was officially "removed" from the nation.

In this way, deportability, detention, and deportation are connected points along a continuum of experience. Those who are detained are locked up, held by force. This control and loss of autonomy circulates throughout different stages of removal: all migrants find themselves trapped or *encerrado* in certain ways. Whether it is ICE agents controlling ordinary citizens through force and intimidation or a judge ruling on the fate of a young man's future, there is a near certainty in these trajectories of detention. Already deemed displaceable, undocumented migrants move through detention toward a likely outcome. This was the case for Jaime as he traveled to the border on that fateful day. He flew from Denver to El Paso and then after a long bus ride arrived at a small border town in the Mexican state of Tamaulipas. The bus entered a fenced-in facility patrolled by still more U.S. agents. There, the officers removed the cuffs—leaving deep, red marks on Jaime's wrists, a trace of how the force of deportation can be embodied physically—opened the gate, and Jaime and the others left the United States. Jaime crossed into Mexico by foot and called his father. "My dad said to get on a bus to my grandmother's town," and so he did.

Deported

"It was very humiliating. There I was in an orange jumpsuit, handcuffed. It was awful." As Carlos retold the details of his detention and deportation, he stared at the ground and spoke softly.[16] He recounted how ashamed he felt throughout the experience of being deported. Carlos's father's death was the impetus for a chain of events that ended with his deportation. When his father died, Carlos felt it was his responsibility to return to his rancho to support his mother and siblings during such a difficult time. He went back to the town where he had grown up—but had not visited since his initial migration—and made arrangements for the burial and helped his mother move into his sister's home. Carlos stayed for several months, and when he tried to go back to his family on the other side of the border, crossing without papers into the United States turned out to be a challenging, and ultimately impossible, endeavor. Carlos attempted to cross five times: once in Laredo, twice in the desert of Sonora, and twice near Ciudad Juárez. The first four crossings resulted in being picked up by U.S. Border Patrol agents and then "returned" to Mexico. The fifth attempt to cross into the United States, however, altered Carlos's trajectory indefinitely.

The fifth and final crossing took place at Ciudad Juárez–El Paso. Carlos went to the border with his nephew, and they arranged to cross with coyotes. The larger group, comprising twenty-seven migrants, was stopped. Carlos's nephew was returned without formal proceedings, as Carlos had been during previous attempts, but Carlos was arrested and transported to Dallas, because, he was told, there was an outstanding warrant for his arrest. Carlos had been arrested the previous year as he was driving to work. When he was pulled over, the police officer said he had turned without signaling. He was given a date for a court appearance and then released. To this day, Carlos remains uncertain about why he was initially arrested for a minor traffic infraction but believes he was racially profiled by police. Because he was undocumented and feared deportation, Carlos never appeared at his hearing. In federal detention, he was given a "choice": wait up to eighteen months for a trial or be deported immediately. Dreading even another minute in detention, he opted for deportation, but he was told that he would not be able to return to the United States for at least ten years. Agents said that if he did return and was caught, he would be imprisoned for a minimum of a decade. For Carlos, eighteen months seemed an eternity, so he signed and was "removed."

After the deportation, Carlos again returned to his hometown in Mexico. He moved back into the family's home, which had been shuttered for over a decade. He was geographically close to his siblings and mother, but his wife and five children were far away, still living in Texas. He started some small improvement projects on his property and hoped to plant pinto beans again as he had nearly two decades before. But, he told me, life changed after deportation. He felt lonely and overwhelmed and—according to his wife, Lucía—suffered from depression. He was ashamed about what had happened. Rumors circulated about late-night socializing, alcohol binges, and infidelities. He broke his arm, making work in the fields that much more challenging. Lucía worried about him constantly.

It is unclear how much of Carlos's depression and difficulties upon return to Mexico were the result of his distance from his family in Dallas and how much may have been caused by his bafflement and incomprehension of the processes by which he ended up in Mexico, although surely both contributed. Processes of removal are framed in the context of certainty or permanence by immigration officials but are nearly always experienced by migrants as obscurity and confusion. Nearly every conversation I have had with deportees about deportation includes bewilderment or perplexity about what precisely happened, the process through which they were removed, how they ended up back in Mexico, and the permanence of their status as one who was returned. Of course, there is no preparing for deportation and its paradoxical effects: even as one fears its imminence it is difficult to imagine in concrete terms. Deportation in its enactment is experienced as having unreal, murky, and even surreal dimensions as well as tangible consequences. In all cases, deportation and its aftermath are alienating, as people with lives firmly connected to the United States see those ties severed in an instant.

The state's removal of foreign nationals can take very different forms. Rodrigo was returned through expedited removal, a form of deportation processed by individual government agents at the nation's borders without a hearing in immigration court or an appearance before a judge. According to the National Immigration Law Center, the use, scope, and territory of expedited removal have expanded significantly since it was first established as part of the U.S. Illegal Immigration Reform and Immigrant Responsibility Act of 1996, making it an increasingly common way for migrants to be deported. On the one hand, those who go through the expedited process are not held for long periods of time in relative isolation. On the other hand, the expedited process gives even fewer opportunities for the migrant to be heard or to produce possible proof of belonging.

Migrants may be removed en masse, as in the deportations carried out under Operation Streamline. Some deportees, like Carlos, are returned after signing a removal order and giving up the right to a hearing in immigration court. Others, like Jaime, choose to remain in detention and wait for a hearing, a process that is often backlogged and can, depending on the circumstances of the case and the region where it is being considered, take months or even years to be completed. Although he is not certain, and no longer has any paperwork related to the removal, it is likely that Miguel was returned through "voluntary return," a form of deportation that does not have the same legal consequences as "removal." Yet as Rodrigo's case proves, individuals can be deported, and thus have formidable sanctions against return to the United States put in place, even while following or trying to follow the law.

. . .

For Federico and Gaby, deportation meant packing up a home and making arrangements for a sudden departure, but it also required gathering up a life of twenty-five years and making choices about what would have to be left behind. Federico and his family parted with nearly everything: "We lost the house, we lost many things. We gave things away. We tried to make arrangements so that we could leave, but, well . . . we lost a lot." Many of the family's losses were material, but, as Federico described, the less tangible losses were far more profound.

Born in a small, rural community in Zacatecas, Mexico, Federico migrated as a young man, in the 1980s, to Los Angeles, California. Several months later, his wife, Gaby, followed, and they made the United States their home, living for more than two decades in Southern California. After spending all of his adult life in the United States as an undocumented migrant, Federico wanted desperately to "fix his papers," to change his status so that he would be authorized to be in the country. Federico was not comfortable living "hidden," so he consulted with an attorney and learned that he was eligible to apply for permanent residency. He felt a deep connection—and had given much—to the nation. As he told me, "I value the way of life in the United States. The United States is a good country." He worked for the same company for sixteen years, had five U.S. citizen children (ages ten to twenty-four at the time), volunteered at prisons through his local parish, and was part of a strong network of family, friends, neighbors, coworkers, and church members.

He began the paperwork to process a change in immigration status for Gaby and himself, but after the applications were submitted, the couple was contacted by U.S. Citizenship and Immigration Services (USCIS) and told that they were not actually eligible to receive green cards. Instead, Federico and Gaby were ordered to leave the country: they were being deported. The couple also learned that the "attorney" who had required advance payment and submitted the applications was not an attorney at all but a notary public. The notary had, erroneously but intentionally, told Federico and Gaby that they were eligible for U.S. permanent residency. They had been the victims of fraud. Like Rodrigo, an effort to obey the law and to do the right thing started a process in motion that had the seemingly inevitable end of deportation.

Federico immediately hired an immigration attorney. However, despite efforts to cancel or defer the removal order, Federico and Gaby were told, five years after first filing for a change of status, that they had to leave the country or face imprisonment. "When the letter arrived informing us that we had to leave, it was very difficult. I thought, 'How am I going to do this? What am I going to do back in Mexico?' After so many years here, so many years that my family lived here . . . " Federico's voice trailed off, his eyes teary. "I feel it was caused by the judge's bad decisions. I'm not saying that we were without fault, but judges should consider the family."

Federico described the time leading up to their departure as very stressful. He and Gaby were told that they needed to leave within sixty days. How does one dismantle a life in a matter of weeks, or in no time at all, as is the case for most deportees? And what replaces it? They closed accounts, said good-bye to family and friends, and wrapped up loose ends as best they could. They lost their home, sold or gave away possessions, and just before their time expired went to Mexico with their five children. They made the decision to return to their rancho in Zacatecas and restart their lives, or—given that the children had never been to Mexico—start completely anew.

Unlike the majority of migrants who are removed by the state, Federico and Gaby were deported without spending time in detention. They were never questioned by U.S. Border Patrol agents or arrested by law enforcement. Just as they were deported while trying to follow the law, so too did they follow the law by "voluntarily" complying with the deportation order. The deportation took place despite the fact that Federico was always law-abiding in every other sense: he wanted to "legalize" and had never had previous problems with law enforcement, "not even a parking ticket." "But," he explained, "my problem was always the papers."

Here, Federico was categorized as and made alien through the very process that he hoped would change his status. Trapped by the state's categorization and removal of particular individuals, Federico and Gaby are among the millions of migrants who, regardless of specific circumstances, face generalizing forms of alienation. This state of being—

encerrado—is engendered by displaceability, as individuals and their families are forced out of the country. In fact, enclosure and banishment are defining characteristics of the state's alienation of migrants. There are those who are marked displaceable, those who may be expelled from the nation. Although "aliens" are assumed to be foreign nationals, displaceability can extend to individuals across generations and regardless of their formal citizenship or national membership.

Departed

When Emy and Manuel made arrangements for their four children, ranging in age from three to fourteen, to cross the U.S.-Mexico border, the children's safety was their priority. They found a respectable coyote, someone they could trust, and made a substantial payment to ensure that the children made it safely to their destination. But this crossing was not a typical one: while most border crossings facilitated by guides involve movement of unauthorized migrants from Mexico to the United States, these children were U.S. citizens who migrated the other direction, from north to south. After Emy was deported, she and Manuel decided that it would be best for the children to join her in Mexico, so they made the necessary arrangements to have a coyote bring the children directly to Emy. Within a day of departing from a border town in Texas, the children and Emy were reunited.

Prior to detention and deportation, Emy had lived primarily in the United States, for a period of more than fifteen years. When a car accident killed her parents and her brother, Emy traveled to Mexico for the funeral and to support her family. After several months in Mexico, she decided it was time to "go back" or "return" to the United States, so she went to the border, intending to cross by land, wading through the Rio Grande/Rio Bravo and walking through the desert. But when she arrived the coyotes told her that there had been a change in plans: because of increasing apprehensions along the border in recent days, Emy would cross with documents supplied by the coyotes, a passport that was valid but belonged to someone else. Emy told me she was very hesitant to cross that way; the photo on the passport looked nothing like her, and the woman was more than twenty years older than Emy. However, because Emy had already paid for her passage and was at the border without family or resources, she went ahead with the crossing. When attempting to enter the United States, however, her fears were actualized: she was stopped and questioned by immigration officials.

They found her "inadmissible" and transferred her to a federal detention center.

Emy's deportation prompted the departure of her four U.S. citizen children. The eldest siblings, teenagers Cora and Joaquín, had been to Mexico as young children but had few memories of their mother's home community. The two younger children had never visited Mexico, so their transnational border crossing was a first. When I spoke with Cora several months after her departure from the United States, she still seemed stunned by the sudden move. One day she was at the mall with friends, and by the end of the week she was in a dusty, rural community in Mexico's countryside. For these children, their mother's deportation meant expulsion from their nation and from their home.

As people are deported, many more depart. Departed U.S. citizens experience what Daniel Kanstroom calls "*de facto* deportations,"[17] removals that are informal or undocumented. Although the movement of Cora and her siblings may not be neatly categorized as forced, it was certainly not voluntary. The family had no other option if the children were to live with Emy. Of course, U.S. citizen children have a right to remain in their nation of origin, but in practical terms, this is likely to be impossible. Toddlers and school-age children cannot parent themselves, and leaving children temporarily with family or friends in the United States raises logistical problems related to custody that are for many insurmountable. Indeed, some parents lose custody of children precisely because they are separated due to detention or deportation.[18] This risk, of the state formally and permanently severing the relationship between parent and child, demonstrates how the departure of loved ones following deportation may be the only option.

Those who depart have different immigration statuses within the United States. Extending Kanstroom's argument, noncitizens can be de facto deported as well. For example, after Carlos was deported, his wife, Lucía, an undocumented migrant at the time, departed. Initially, Lucía felt it was best for her to stay in Texas and keep working. More than ever, the family depended on her income. But then one day, Carlos called Lucía to say that he was going to sell the house and their land "so that he could keep drinking." Lucía was shocked and knew she had to take action: "I had to come back." Lucía and the couple's two youngest children, Eduardo and Nico, packed up and moved south. Their departure, like Carlos's deportation, was chaotic despite being seemingly self-initiated. Within a few weeks of the alarming phone call that had prompted Lucía's departure, she and her sons were on a bus, "returning" to Mexico.

Lucía was essentially de facto deported, through a kind of undocumented deportation, because of or in response to her husband's deportation. She experienced return in much the same way her husband did, returning after more than a decade to the community where she grew up and the nation where she was born. Their sons were also among the departed. An undocumented migrant, Eduardo, like Lucía, was informally deported back to his nation of origin, but, unlike his parents, he went "back" to a place he did not know. Their youngest son, Nico, a U.S. citizen, was de facto deported, departing from the nation of his birth. Because of his parents' undocumented status in the United States, he had never traveled to Mexico prior to his father's deportation. When the state removed Carlos, it effectively banished Lucía, Eduardo, and Nico as well. These are among the unrecorded, "forced" departures that result from deportation. The departed may go intentionally or even after lengthy planning, but this does not make north-south movement a matter of choice.

Finally, the departed also include those who are not deported but who are sent back by USCIS, typically to wait during the processing of a status change. For example, when Pablo married a U.S. citizen, Laura, he thought that a change in status would be relatively easy. However, when the couple had an appointment with USCIS, they were told that Pablo would need to return to Mexico while the paperwork was finalized. His departure was devastating for the family. Initially, Laura and their three children traveled with him to the rancho where he had grown up. They stayed for two weeks, but because Laura needed to return to work, she was unable to extend her stay. Pablo remained in the rancho with his mother, thinking that his time in Mexico would be brief. The months, however, became years, and Pablo, Laura, and their children were forced to live apart much longer than anticipated. After nearly three years, Pablo finally received word from USCIS that he could travel to the border to complete paperwork and be interviewed by immigration officials. He again departed, this time for the United States.

Undocumented migrants are labeled "deportable," but through deportability and its accompanying displaceability, the state casts a wide net. Beyond those deported, there are millions who must depart. Through family ties, many more than those legally deemed "alien" are constructed as displaceable, not fully part of the nation. It is not only deportees who are affected by deportation and not only foreign nationals who are *encerrado,* or enclosed, by U.S. immigration and deportation policies. Increasingly, all must navigate a climate of deportability and the displaceability of alienation.

· · ·

On a flight to Mexico City departing from Phoenix, Arizona, I witnessed U.S. Border Patrol agents stationed along the walkway as passengers boarded the plane. They would occasionally stop someone—those I saw were young men of color—and ask for identification. Notably, this was after the very lengthy and thorough Transit Security Administration screening required to board any plane in the United States today. After watching the agents approach several people in front of and behind me, I asked one of the officers why the U.S. Border Patrol would want to check the papers of people traveling to Mexico. He immediately responded, with a raised voice, "We have authority here! We are in U.S. territory." "Certainly," I replied, but I was still confused about the logic of inspecting the documents of those *leaving* the country. "Honestly, we are protecting you," he said as he smiled. "We are checking for weapons, for pedophiles."

I boarded the plane (without further inspection) but was reminded of what several migrants had told me: *la migra* will get you coming and going. During my research, one woman asked if I had heard of those who were deported as they departed, formally deported while crossing south at the U.S.-Mexico border. Although I have not interviewed migrants who were deported this way, as I watched the U.S. Border Patrol agents checking passports far from the border itself, the woman's cautionary tale seemed more plausible than I had initially thought. On the one hand, the DHS's deportation of people as they return may be a strategy to deter undocumented migration. On the other hand, it is almost certainly a way to further assert control over members and non-members of the nation, especially if my own interaction with an agent is anything to go by. Regardless of whether this was the case, however, one point was certain: departures can be converted into deportations, even if not officially.

DISAPPEARANCE

One afternoon in Mexico, when I stopped by to visit my friend Blanca, she called me into the living room and proudly introduced me to her daughter-in-law, Jasmin, and her two grandchildren. Jasmin and the children first spoke with me in English and then, so that Blanca could understand, alternated between English and Spanish. Jasmin and her daughters are, I quickly learned, U.S. citizens. Jasmin explained that because her husband—Blanca's son, Ignacio, whom the family calls Nacho—is an undocumented migrant in the United States, Jasmin and the children often travel to Mexico without him "so that the children can spend time with their family." As Jasmin described it, the risks are too great to have Nacho join them. A border crossing and attempted reentry into the United States could result in detention and deportation, so the family arranges for Jasmin and the girls to make the trip without him. Blanca told me that it has been difficult not to see her son for so many years but that the visits from Jasmin and her grandchildren are a joy.

Because Jasmin is a U.S. citizen, Nacho is, in theory, eligible for U.S. residency and eventual naturalization as a citizen. Jasmin explained that after marrying, they immediately filed the papers to change his status but soon discovered that the process was not going to be as straightforward as they had hoped. Because Nacho had entered the country and resided there for many years without papers, immigration agents told the couple that Nacho—like Pablo—would have to leave the United States for a period. In Nacho's case, he was told that he would be required to return to Mexico for a minimum of ten years. This penalty was, in Jasmin's words, the "*castigo*," or punishment, that they faced. And a severe punishment it was: the newlyweds, expecting a baby, could not bear the idea of being apart for a decade. "How is that a marriage?," she asked. She wondered how the government could expect families to live like that.

"So one day," continued Jasmin, "my husband simply disappeared." She said that faced with a decade of separation that would irreparably strain the family, they decided that Nacho would stay in the United States but "disappear." They would live their lives as though he had gone back to Mexico. Jasmin went on to describe what such a disappearance means for the family: "He doesn't use his real name. It is like he isn't there. It is as though my husband doesn't exist. We are living as though he is in Mexico. He had to disappear." She explained that after the ten years required by the government—it had been six so far—Nacho would reappear, or "come back" to the United States, and file the necessary papers after his supposed decade away. As Jasmin described it, he would "*arreglar sus papeles,*" meaning that he would submit any necessary papers or documents at that time. Tellingly, *arreglar* can mean "to fix," "to sort out," or "to put in order." In the

[handwritten marginal note: Argument: The U.S. foreign policy disregards legitimate methods of naturalization]

experience of Nacho and Jasmin, ensuring order amid the chaos of deportability requires waiting—putting life on hold while life goes on.

As the experiences of those touched by removal—both its threat and its actualization—make clear, deportation is linked to and results in disappearances of many sorts. Through relatedness and ties to others, nearly all, regardless of citizenship or immigration status, are at risk of "disappearing." Jaime and Miguel, when detained, disappeared from the social fabric of their communities, caught in a structure that produces "disappearing parents"[19] and "unseen prisoners."[20] Following the workplace raids and audits in Reno, the targeted migrants vanished; far more people disappeared from the community, fleeing to unknown destinations. Of course, deportees—such as Federico and Gaby, Carlos, and Emy—disappear from daily life in the United States, sometimes after decades of calling the country their home. Each day in Tucson, seventy people disappear into detention and then are expelled from the United States, disappearing from the country they had hoped to reach as migrants. Similarly, there are those who disappear from the United States with deported loved ones, departing unexpectedly from networks of family and friends.

Disappearances from life in the United States may be actual—such as those of Pablo, Emy's children, and Carlos's family—or virtual—as is Nacho's. Virtual or not, Nacho's wife and children, U.S. citizens who continue to live in the United States, feel the effects of his disappearance, and if Nacho were to be discovered by immigration officials, the disappearance of all family members would be likely. There are those who preemptively return or, in the case of small children, those who are preemptively returned to Mexico because of their parents' well-founded fear of deportation, and those who, like Fátima and David, stay in the United States and are forced to become invisible because of their undocumented status in the nation. Deportation and displacement can cause migrants to vanish to Mexico or within the United States, to experience phantom or reluctant returns to either country, and to move between spaces of presence and absence with unsettling speed and uncertainty.

Those who disappear because of deportation remind us that beyond the individuals who are formally deported, many more are caught up in deportation policies and proceedings—confined, restricted, and controlled by global landscapes of state power. Deportees are not alone in assuming futures shaped by narrowing options. Those I have discussed in this chapter—those who live with deportability, those who are deported, those who have departed—are all constructed as "displaceable" by the state. Alienation and displaceability not only attaches to different individuals and their family members and networks, but moves through communities, as millions of people with diverse U.S. immigration statuses are caught within transnational migrations and especially forced returns. In this sense, all migrants who are marked "deportable"—and all individuals connected to those labeled as such—are alienated by immigration and deportation laws. People are both trapped and expelled as they disappear and are disappeared through state action. Limited autonomous movement, increasing immobility, forced mobility, and/or banishment make up the many experiences of those affected by deportation in the current moment.

The alienation of deportation takes different forms and is enacted through stages of disappearance outlined here: displaceability, deportability, detention, deportation, departure. Regardless of status, many find themselves returned, returning against their will, or "returning" for the first time. The state extends alienation through family relations, as kinship shapes exclusion and individuals are made "alien" in ways much like their loved ones are, even if their own statuses differ, attaching alienation to far more than only those who are deported. The multiple displacements and disappearances that result from removal, as millions are made invisible or swiftly disappear from daily life in the United States, share the quality of being deeply dehumanizing. The invisibility and enclosure of undocumented migrants produce and stem from these very disappearances. In the end, deportation and its resulting departures create chaos for those near and far.

CHAPTER 3

Violation

I thought I was going to kill myself . . . I'm used to my
independence, and suddenly I was like a caged animal.

—Emy

As Dina related what had happened in her rural Mexican town just two
weeks earlier, her voice became hushed: "They say nine people were
killed, but no one can be certain. They don't report the deaths of sol-
diers or *narcos* [members of drug cartels]." She went on to describe how
three of the "civilians" who died that night were children: a nine-year-
old girl and a teenaged couple who were in their final year at the local
high school. Her depiction was vivid, the details terrifying. On a Friday
evening, there had been a shootout on the main plaza—a spot that bus-
tles with activity at that time—between members of the military and
narcos after a confrontation at a *quinceañera* (fifteenth birthday party)
in a nearby town. The nine-year-old was waiting in the car while her
mother bought her an ice cream cone. The young couple had been planning a summer wedding to follow their high school graduation, scheduled to take place later that month. Traumatized, a woman selling tam-
ales in the plaza who had witnessed the deaths quit working immediately;
according to Dina, she refused to go back to the town's center. The community had been taken over by fear.[1]

Despite the transnational political and economic structures that led
to the escalation of the "drug war," according to all accounts the violence had begun suddenly. Almost overnight it seemed that violence was
"everywhere." Dina explained that members of the cartels had recently
moved to the area and lived just a few blocks from her. "*Los malos,*" or
bad people, as she called them, were now controlling or overseeing

nearly all economic enterprises, from the local gas station and small grocery stands to large moneymakers such as alcohol sales at parties in the region, like the event that had precipitated the shootout that night. Towns that were once described as quiet and friendly were now haunted by suspicion and terror. The "*inseguridad* [insecurity]," as it is labeled by people throughout Mexico, felt foreign and unsettling to everyone who spoke of it.[2] The violence seemed to be uncontrollable: the military, law enforcement, and politicians were unable, or in some cases unwilling, to stop it. Insecurity was the new norm.

But there was another form of violence also plaguing these communities: the detention and deportation of migrants living in the United States. As mentioned, prior to 2008, I knew of very few migrants who had been deported, despite years of research with hundreds of people who had crossed the border and lived in the United States without authorization. Now, however, locals told me of the many migrants who had been "sent back," and deportees described the terror of the removal process, including interactions with law enforcement in the United States and time in U.S. detention centers. People who under any other circumstances would likely never be incarcerated were now experiencing the violence of a well-funded and expansive prison complex.

Although drug war violence and the violence of return are typically understood as separate issues, these ostensibly very different forms of violence frequently intersect. For example, the father of the young girl who was killed in the plaza was an undocumented migrant in the United States. Fearing the dangers of traveling to Mexico and then attempting to migrate north once more, as well as the increased risk of deportation and detention whenever moving transnationally, he decided he would not return to Mexico for his daughter's funeral. He and his family felt that the risk of more suffering and tragedy was too great. The convergence of these forms of violence intensifies the already acute instability and insecurity in the lives of transnational Mexicans.

Thus violence is increasingly layered on deportation, itself a violent process, so that those who are removed from the nation face insecurity in multiple and additional contexts. As individuals and families migrate or are forced to move both north and south, they witness and experience the "transnational circulation of violence."[3] Violence may take diverse forms and occur in different settings, but as these violations of safety connect across borders they highlight the ways that violence is frequently the condition of transnational lives. The context of deportation sharpens this conclusion in that chaos and violation shape lives before, during, and after removal.

THE TRANSNATIONAL CIRCULATION OF VIOLENCE

At an art museum in the city of Zacatecas, I met a local, an elderly Zacatecano, who asked what had brought me to the area. I briefly explained my research as a study about deportation and return migration and said that I wanted to understand how such movement was affecting families and communities. He nodded, said he understood why such research should be conducted, and then asked if he could share a joke with me. Intrigued that my research topic would elicit humor, I said, of course, I would like to hear it. He sat down on a bench and related the following.

> The prime minister of the United Kingdom, the president of the United States, and the president of Mexico went on a diplomatic trip together to visit Heaven and Hell. In Hell, they asked the Devil if they could use the telephone to check in on their respective countries, offering to pay the cost of the long-distance calls. First, the British prime minister called his country; he spoke for a few minutes and was relieved to know that all was fine at home. When he hung up, the Devil said that the call would cost £100, which the prime minister promptly paid. Next, the president of the United States called home and also spoke briefly—no problems to report. The cost of his call: $100. Finally, the president of Mexico called his country. He was on the line for nearly an hour as his advisers spoke of widespread violence, profound insecurity, and enduring poverty. He hung up the phone, the difficulties of Mexico weighing heavily. "One peso," said the Devil. "But how can the call cost so little when I spoke for so long?," asked the Mexican president. The Devil was quick to respond, "Mr. President, with all due respect, for you, Hell is a local call."

The elder's commentary in the form of a joke spoke volumes: he linked the deportation of Mexican nationals from the United States to the violence and insecurity that Mexico faced. As I reflected on the words and experiences of returnees, it became clear that these seemingly distinct processes were indeed intertwined.

Beginning in the 2000s, drug violence in Mexico started to escalate just as the United States began deporting Mexican nationals in record numbers. Tens of thousands of people have been killed in Mexico due to drug violence; more than two million individuals have been deported from the United States under the Obama administration, thousands have died at the border attempting to cross, and there has been a growing number of deaths of detainees while in U.S. custody in recent years. While diverse conditions shape these different settings, for transnational Mexicans such manifestations of violence converge, creating a climate of insecurity. This is "fear as a way of life."[4] In Mexico, terror is unpredictable and widespread: people disappear and are victims of horrific acts. In the United States, Mexicans also live with unpredictability: they face the constant fear of deportation and potential "disappearances"—albeit of a very different form from those that stem from drug violence—as migrants are taken from their homes and workplaces and removed from the nation.

Violence and vulnerability exist and move transnationally. Violence in the different settings I describe—violence of seemingly different forms—is not simply coincidental but mutually constitutive. Violence moves through families and communities, geographically while crossing the U.S.-Mexico border and temporally across generations, linking individuals and violent acts in ways that may not be initially or clearly evident. Early on during fieldwork, I discovered that the study of deportation could not be separated from an analysis of violence. While some of the violence accompanying deportation and removal is evident in the processes of alienation and alienization documented in the previous chapter, less overtly linked to these processes are other forms and contexts of violence faced by the deported and their affective networks.

The nature of this violence "defies easy categorization,"[5] making it difficult to disimbricate multiple forms of violence registered by those who are affected. As Nancy Scheper-Hughes and Philippe Bourgois outline, one cannot always tease out distinct forms of violence; instead of categorizing violence as discrete, disconnected acts, they propose a "continuum of violence" along which different but related forms of violence can be plotted, ranging from genocide to "everyday" violence that stems from poverty or racial inequality.[6] Scheper-Hughes and Bourgois do not aim to conflate diverse violent acts but instead to demonstrate how conceptualizing violence along a continuum can bring both commonalities and differences into relief. The model of a continuum of violence is useful for locating potentially obscured but shared causalities and identifying layers of violence that make their effect particularly devastating.

In the case of deportation, the innately violent acts of alienation and return may introduce other forms of violence, such as when a migrant is deported to a community plagued by killings. One of the disconcerting questions related to violence is what makes these horrific acts possible.[7]

All too often, violence begins with the devaluation or dehumanization of certain people—common to the processes of shaming and alieniza-tion—and ends with unimaginable atrocities,[8] underscoring that while particular forms and various degrees of cruelty exist, violent acts can be of a kind and of a context.

As a result of state actions and, in particular, deportations, transna-tional subjects are exposed to violence in multiple forms—direct and indirect,[9] physical and symbolic,[10] structural,[11] and cultural[12]—although much of it goes unrecognized or at least untraced to its sources. As Coutin outlines, even the supposed "neutrality" of the word *removal*—the legal term for a deportation—"hides the violence that removal wreaks on individuals, families, communities."[13] Diverse forms of vio-lence are the product of, but can also perpetuate or intensify, immigra-tion controls and enforcement.

The vulnerability and violations that people face stem from a broader context. As a condition of the "materiality of the social,"[14] material relations are intertwined with suffering.[15] Thus research on structural violence can "inform the study of the social machinery of oppression."[16] The structural and cultural violence that shapes the lives of transna-tional Mexicans is a reflection of the poverty that drives migration to begin with, as the man expressed in his joke that day. Recognition of violence as a continuum or interconnected, transnational web of acts underscores forms of violence that are "exerted systematically—that is, indirectly—by everyone who belongs to a certain social order."[17] The violence of the U.S. immigration regime is increasingly present in the lives of people in the U.S.-Mexico transnation. The transnational circu-lation of violence is manifested both directly and indirectly: physical violence defines the border that separates kin and prevents reunifica-tion, while structural violence reaches into the personal lives and inti-mate exchanges of families in a transnational space.

INSECURITIES

News headlines such as "A Deadly 24 Hours in Mexico" and "In Mex-ico, Mass Graves Found with 59 Bodies" depict Mexico as an undoubt-edly violent place. Transnational Mexicans face many insecurities, not only in Mexico, where such violence is increasingly seen as common or even expected, but also just north of the border and within the United States, spaces that many view in sharp contrast to Mexico as it is depicted in the media. While violence in Mexico is indeed horrific and unprecedented in many ways, the generalized insecurity that transnational subjects experience is not limited to Mexican territory and is not only related to the drug economy. Insecurity takes multiple forms in both Mexico and the United States, and it is also present while migrants move between the two countries. In a transnational context, there are multiple forms of intersectional insecurity: the insecurity that people directly experience; insecurity and its aftermath that people witness; stories of insecurity that, like violence itself, circulate. I turn to these insecurities to show how they can be difficult to delink as experienced in everyday lives.

Inseguridad en México

In the working-class neighborhood where I lived for a period in the city of Zacatecas, the daytime was filled with activity: streets bustling with cart vendors, the chimes of the garbage collector, trucks selling tanks of natural gas and announcing their arrival on a loudspeaker, church bells that marked each hour. At night, all was quiet and still. However, on one deadly night, gunfire erupted in the early morning, around 4:00 a.m., and did not stop for nearly a half hour. The target was the home of a family with two young daughters, a family in which the father was allegedly involved in drug trafficking. The family disappeared, the bodies taken from the scene by the perpetrators. What neighbors found especially disconcerting is that no one—not the military, not law enforcement—came to the house for hours, despite multiple calls to emergency services. As one woman described it, no one came until the shooting had long subsided, when all was quiet again and the perpetrators and victims of the shooting had vanished from the scene.

"Mexico is a lawless place," explained Tito, a naturalized U.S. citizen born in Mexico who has lived in the United States for more than thirty years. When we talked about the violence throughout the region, he described *"un pueblo sin ley,"* meaning both a place and a people without law. With events such as the shooting in a neighborhood in Zacatecas and the battle between military and *narcos* in a once-quiet town plaza, Mexico did indeed seem to be lawless, slipping into a state of chaos, punctuated by an absence of those who enforce the laws. Even a military checkpoint that had been on the highway to Monterrey near one of my field sites for more than a decade was no longer there. Now, stories of *inseguridad*—and insecurity itself—swirled around everyday exchanges, proliferating as if everywhere.

[handwritten margin note: opportunity to move the reader but doesn't]

Although the violence in Mexico is concentrated in particular regions, especially in disputed territories and along the northern border, it is increasingly part of everyday experience throughout the country, or, in the words of Veena Das, "in the weave of life."[18] While in office between 2006 and 2012, Mexican president Felipe Calderón declared, "It's a war,"[19] and the death toll has certainly reflected this sentiment. Estimates of the number of people killed by drug trade violence under Calderón's six-year presidency range from 47,515[20] to 120,000 or more.[21] A Mexican government agency, the Sistema Nacional de Seguridad Pública, reported that in the first eight months of President Enrique Peña Nieto's administration, there were 12,598 homicides (an average of 52 deaths each day), 1,032 kidnappings, 5,242 cases of extortion, and 90,202 violent carjackings.[22] While reports of the number of killings vary widely, even "official" figures—which are disputed by watch groups and widely understood to fall far short of the actual death toll—reflect an undeniably profound loss of life. Bombs detonated in marketplaces, shootings in public spaces, beheadings, disappearances, assassinations of politicians and journalists, and the growing number of victims who are not employed by drug cartels make evident that violence is part of everyday experience throughout Mexico.[23]

My research on deportation was framed by these stories of violence and danger. Indeed, virtually every visit to a town or family included a recounting of an event that had threatened the "*tranquilidad*" that residents had previously associated with their home. After relating the shooting in the plaza, Dina invited me to accompany her to the center of town while she ran errands. Even this brief trip to pick up groceries was filled with stories of threats to the community. While we were waiting at one shop, several young men walked by, hipsters in pegged jeans who seemed out of place in this rural setting. Later, as we walked to the car, Dina's teenage daughter told me that we had just passed a drug dealer. "How do you know?," I asked. "You just know," she replied. "Everybody knows." "And the young men we saw earlier?," I wondered. "Yes," Dina said. "They are also *malos*. They are 'scorpions'— lookouts, vigilantes who work for the *narcos*. They are bad people, very dangerous." On our ride home, Dina pointed out the one house in the neighborhood "with permission to sell drugs," where "all kinds of people buy"—men and women, people of all ages.

As we drove out of town, headed to a wedding in a neighboring rancho, Dina continued her description of threats to the community, almost as though she were a tour guide but one whose job was to point out disaster and devastation. She nodded toward a gas station where the owner had been beaten a few months earlier after refusing to make monthly payments to the *narcos*. When we arrived at the wedding, the stories of violence continued. The grandson of an elderly woman had been stopped by a group of men while driving alone on an isolated dirt road; he had been carjacked, beaten, and robbed. Weeks later, he received a mysterious phone call, offering a deal: meet at a prearranged site, pay a large sum of money, and he would have his new truck back. His mother refused to let him go.

Even the wedding we attended ended with a fight in which both men were seriously injured; they were lucky, one woman explained, that no one died, as had a young man a few months earlier after a similar fight at another event. At a local celebration for Mexican Independence Day, I was startled to see masked guards with automatic weapons at each entrance to the dance hall; when I asked about them, several residents confirmed that they had been hired for "safety," to make the event more "secure." People tried to joke about the violence—such as when a woman said that her hard-of-hearing mother-in-law kept referring to one cartel, the Zetas, as the *"tetas"* (nipples or tits)—but everyone seemed aware that there was no way to make light of the situation. There seemed to be no escaping the *inseguridad*.

Insecurity in the United States and the Transnation

When Tito described Mexico as "lawless," he compared it to the United States: "In Mexico, it isn't like it is here in the U.S. Here, you have laws, people are protected in ways they are not in Mexico. The police are here to help people." "Well," interrupted his wife, Amanda, "they don't help everyone. We aren't like you. If we do something wrong, it's different." As their focus moved from Mexico to the United States, they talked about how migrants north of the border are likely to be treated differently than gringos by law enforcement and *la migra*. Tito and Amanda had recently experienced the trauma of deportation in their own family when a number of family members had been deported in separate cases— including their nephew and brother-in-law—and Amanda deeply missed her sister, who had returned to Mexico when her husband had to leave. Their stories revealed that the United States, like Mexico, can be a frightening and insecure place for many in the community. As Tito and Amanda talked about fear in both countries, it became clear that, especially for those without documents, the violence was indeed inescapable.

Contexts of violence in Mexico and the United States are inter-twined—historically, politically, and economically. The drug trade is, of course, inherently transnational, as supply from the south moves through violent channels to meet the demands of markets in the north. Conversely, weapons move from north to south, exacerbating the violence. There is also a history of the U.S. government simultaneously recruiting Mexican labor and expelling Mexican nationals by force. In addition, financial hardship from the economic crisis is perceived as extending transnationally. Migrants often make this connection in their personal narratives. As one man told me, referring to economic recession, "The United States has a cold, but Mexico has pneumonia. We are very poor here in Mexico . . . that is why there is violence." On both sides of the border, the drug trade and growing violence can be read as a symptom of poverty, often the impetus for movement from south to north in the first place.

One of the most obvious connections between seemingly disparate violent forms is the ways that migrants are uniquely caught in the violence or even specifically targeted. There are increasingly risks to migrants *as migrants,* vulnerabilities that stem from their identities as individuals who migrate through Mexico or between Mexico and the United States, or as members of transnational families or networks. The discovery of the bodies of seventy-two murdered migrants in the Mexican state of Tamaulipas in August 2010—what is considered among the worst massacres of migrants in Mexico—viscerally demonstrates the vulnerabilities of those migrating as laborers. In events like these, the violence of migration and the violation of the drug war converge, shaping transnational lives before migrants even reach U.S. territory. The drug war's violence and kidnappings also generate new flows to the north—producing "drug war refugees"[24]—and result in migrations that may place transnational subjects at even greater risk. Violence is also reducing the voluntary return migration of Mexican nationals to their home communities as both the journey and the destination are perceived as being more dangerous. As fewer people choose to return, those who are forcibly returned through deportation are increasingly vulnerable to violence.

Migrants and their family members, then, are exposed in particular ways and may even be at risk explicitly because of their connections to and in the United States. Consider, for example, the situation of Vicente, a successful entrepreneur and the owner of one of the larger shops in his small Mexican town.[25] He became scared after he was repeatedly threatened that he or his wife, Tomasita, would be hurt or kidnapped. The couple felt that they were targeted because they were people with resources and, significantly, because they were migrants; they have two adult children living in the United States, and they themselves have traveled to the United States for extended stays several times in recent years. Fearing for their safety, Vicente and Tomasita traveled on tourist visas to the United States to wait out the threats. This couple, however, had options that most transnational Mexicans do not, since tourist visas are very difficult for rural Mexicans to obtain and frequent travel between Mexico and the United States requires resources that many migrants do not have.

Such threatened or actualized kidnappings are becoming uncomfortably common throughout the transnation, with migrants and their family members often at the center of this form of intimidation. As Rodolfo García Zamora, a professor of development studies at the Universidad Autónoma de Zacatecas, has explained, "The relatives of Mexicans in the United States have become a new profit center for Mexico's crime industry. . . . Hundreds of families are emigrating out of fear of kidnap or extortion."[26] For example, in a town in the state of Zacatecas, an elderly farmer—in his eighties—was kidnapped and tortured.[27] The kidnappers contacted his daughter, a migrant who was living in the United States, and she wired money to cover the ransom. I know of a similar case in which an elderly man with family members living in Nevada was kidnapped and his adult children were contacted to pay to secure his release. As reported in the New York Times, there is the phone call that "families fear,"[28] someone making contact with migrants in the United States after kidnapping a loved one in Mexico. That some family members in the United States who are contacted to pay a ransom may be deportable renders them unable to ask authorities for help. Just as their presence in the United States makes the kidnapped relative in Mexico a desirable target, since it signals economic advantage, their marginalization and isolation make migrants desirable because they often have no option other than to pay.

Unauthorized border crossings have long been framed by violence, but as drug violence has escalated, so, too, has the violence of passage into the United States. Killings in cities along the border are especially pronounced. Ciudad Juárez—just across the border from El Paso and a major point of entry to the United States—was labeled "the murder capital of the world" at the height of the violence there. Uninhabited stretches of the border make for dangerous, even fatal border crossings.

An already militarized border has become even more so, with violent exchanges occurring daily between migrants and agents on both sides of the border.

Miguel's experience of multiple "detentions" shows how violence continues or can even intensify for migrants as they move north and within the United States. Miguel was subjected to violence by numerous actors in institutions that facilitate and aim to prevent unauthorized migrations: coyotes, employees of smuggler rings that extend into the United States, local law enforcement in U.S. communities, and U.S. Border Patrol and ICE agents. Migrants who have crossed by foot in recent years report having to pay additional fees at various points along the trail to ensure passage as they attempt entry into the United States, and people of all ages, including children,[29] are subject to kidnappings as they cross the border. Death can come to define migration at the border,[30] as more and more migrants go missing in the desert and the number of unidentified bodies grows.

The border is also understood to be a space that is dangerous when moving either direction. Jasmin described how her crossing south into Mexico, at Laredo, Texas, was framed by fear. She and her daughters traveled from Albuquerque to Mexico with a close family friend, a man from a neighboring rancho. Because of the *inseguridad,* they drove first across Texas, rather than crossing at Ciudad Juárez, which would have been the most direct route. Jasmin said that at the border Mexican immigration officials hassled her and her family. In an intimidating exchange, they told her that she did not have the correct paperwork for her U.S. citizen children to enter Mexico. After pleading with them and explaining that they could not easily travel back to New Mexico for the documents, the Mexican agents allowed the family to enter the country.

In the United States, violence is a significant part of the landscape, especially due to the growing deportation regime. Again using the model of a "violence continuum," violent settings in this age of deportation can be tracked through various spaces or encounters: the highly militarized border and the dangers posed to individuals crossing it; the threat of deportation and the inevitable fear that accompanies it; the compromised rights of migrant laborers in diverse industries and domestic spaces; growing nativism and racism; local, state, and federal legislation that intensifies and racializes policing throughout the nation; the incarceration of migrants in immigration detention and criminal justice facilities; and the removal of foreign nationals to and through border zones. Yet as I hope to have shown, the violent spaces that threaten Mexican nationals in the United States are both linked to and exacerbating violence in Mexico, and vice versa, with the result that violence circulates within a transnational space. Thus the violence migrants might experience in the institutional processes of determining and acting on deportability—incarceration, depersonalization, and more—does not end when they reach the end of those processes or are expelled by the state. Rather, deportation opens migrants up to further and new violence and vulnerability.

As discussed, deportability in the United States breeds deep fear, described by migrants in similar fashion to the way people in Mexico describe the insecurity precipitated by the drug wars. As Fátima and David explained, the risk of deportation is a form of violence that one cannot escape. Local and state governments throughout the United States have proposed and passed legislation that stems from nativist or racist assumptions. Such legislation often calls on public officials, including law enforcement officers, teachers, and government administrators (such as clerks at the Department of Motor Vehicles), to identify and report those "suspected" of being in the country without documentation. Civil rights groups, including the American Civil Liberties Union, are tracking the growing number of cases of racial profiling and hate crimes in which immigrants and U.S. citizens of color are specifically targeted. Racially motivated violence and the threat of deportation converge to make the United States a dangerous place for those perceived as being from elsewhere.

Detention and deportation are inherently violent, as individuals are contained, incarcerated, and prevented from moving or forced to move across international boundaries. Detention facilities are profoundly violent spaces, places in which armed guards, shackles, force, and lockdown are used consistently regardless of the reason for one's detention. As in Jaime's case, insecurities can range from time spent in jails and federal immigration detention centers to the demoralizing use of physical restraints during transport and in courtroom settings. Migrants report that U.S. agents consistently follow these protocols, even in cases when migrants are detained only for undocumented presence. Scholars have also found similar practices and conditions when minors are detained.[31] Migrants describe insecurities during detention or while being questioned or transported by federal agents. For example, Rodrigo related that his interactions with U.S. Border Patrol agents was so intimidating that he felt pressured to sign so that he and his wife could escape the interrogation by U.S. agents.

Other forms of violation are more direct. Immigration detention in the United States and the process of removal itself can be especially violent. One young man, Lucas, who was detained as a teenager and spent time in a county jail, told me that he tries not to think about the horrific conditions of his imprisonment; he witnessed the aftermath of two suicides while detained—a cellmate who hung himself and a man who jumped to his death from a second-floor walkway. Lucas was also brutally beaten by a fellow inmate because, he speculated, he was so young. These are images that he fears he will never forget. Back in Mexico, Lucas was approached by members of a powerful local drug cartel about the possibility of employment; he said that his time in a U.S. prison likely made him a desirable recruit. He politely declined. For Lucas, violence is embodied literally. Not only were his autonomy and freedom of movement stripped away and not only does he bear psychological and physical scars, but his experience marks him in such a way that his past is legible on his person—in this case making him vulnerable to potentially violent recruitment to lawlessness.

Emy described detention as "one of the most horrible moments" she had ever experienced. It was devastating to go from being a law-abiding mother and housewife to being a "caged animal." Prior to the deportation, Emy, one of the few women in her community to migrate autonomously, always approached life's challenges with an optimistic attitude: "*Ni modo*" (Oh well), was a common response if someone questioned her choices or lifestyle. But detention and the subsequent deportation were a violation that had worn her down. After just a few short days in a facility in Texas, she said that she thought she might "go crazy." She told me that she contemplated suicide, an act that was previously inconceivable to her. In fact, there are growing numbers of deaths of migrants while in custody, detention, and/or at the hand of U.S. agents.[32] And when migrants are released to violent cities along the U.S.-Mexico border and return to communities in Mexico that are struggling with insecurity, violation continues, intensified or even perpetuated because of the U.S. removal of foreign nationals.

In/security and Il/legality

As Tito and Amanda spoke of violence in two very different contexts, I was struck by the ways that perceptions of lawlessness and law enforcement intertwine to create profound insecurity in migrants' lives. At first, Tito and Amanda said that Mexico was a lawless place, comparing it to the United States—a place where, they said, law and order reign. But as they continued, this distinction became less tenable. For example, Tito explained that a cousin had been deported after being cited for drunk driving. Tito said that his cousin had committed a "crime [*delito*]," so his deportation was perhaps understandable. Yet *delito* can also signal a mistake or an error, and it was also this sense of the word that Tito evoked. Did their cousin deserve to be deported? In some ways he felt, yes, he did, because he had committed an act that was against the law, but in another sense, no—after all, many U.S. citizens are arrested for DWIs but do not similarly have their lives upended.

The couple described others who had been deported or were at risk of deportation. Some had broken the law in their opinion, but they also described several migrants whose only crime was a lack of documentation. True, many of their friends and family members are undocumented, explained Amanda, but that seemed different from committing a "real" crime. Their sister-in-law, for example, was in the United States without authorization. She was filing for DACA (Deferred Action for Childhood Arrivals), and the family hoped her application would be successful. Amanda told me that her sister-in-law was a model citizen in every sense—except her immigration status—so even though she was committing a crime by some definitions, it was difficult to see her as a "criminal."

Throughout our conversation, as Tito and Amanda spoke of violent conditions in Mexico and the United States, they moved back and forth between this discussion of "lawlessness" and "the law," revealing the ways that, regardless of immigration status or citizenship, transnational Mexicans' relation to "the law" is an ambivalent one. In this milieu of violence and insecurity, migrants link lawlessness and the heavy hand of the law. While and after crossing north, "the law" is all around transnational subjects, and yet the United States can be much like a lawless space for migrants and those connected to them, particularly since protections guaranteed by law are not always extended in practice to those who are not formal citizens. Indeed, the violence that accompanies the production of "illegality" in the United States—enacted through policing, deportability, detention, and deportation—also presents clear danger to migrants and contributes to the growing insecurity that frames transnational lives. Here, an environment defined by a constant presence and assertion of "the law" can quickly transform into a climate resembling "lawlessness."

Similar to the contradictions of il/legality and in/security—this conundrum of "the law" and "lawlessness" that Tito described—there are contradictory elements in the narratives about il/legality and im/morality in the lives of those affected by deportation. In public debate about U.S. immigration policy, people often assume a direct correlation between immorality and illegality, and morality and legality, yet there is a kind of violence in the moral judgments that are attached to these categories. Furthermore, the dichotomies fall short in explaining and delineating the range of acts on the part of government actors and migrants. Finally, transnational Mexicans describe the immorality of state action against them: the governments justifies force because migrants are constructed as criminals, a label that is itself produced through violent acts.

These dualities, of legality-morality on the one hand and illegality-immorality on the other, do not necessarily correspond and may not accurately define the experiences of those who cross borders and are expelled from the nation. In fact, as migrants describe the parameters of migration and return, they speak of another inversion: the morality of "illegality" and the immorality of "legality" in the form of policy and its implementation. For those affected by deportation, laws and morality are often disconnected, or at least not connected in the way that the state links the two. "The law" does indeed create contradictions, as migrants and deportees are subject to insecurity by the very governing body that aims to foster security for the nation.

The state carries out deportation through the criminalization of immigrants—criminalization of a new magnitude. As the anthropologist Jonathan Xavier Inda argues, the state's agenda includes "making ethical subjects" through technologies that "call upon citizens to conduct themselves ethically."[33] Unauthorized migrants are, by the state's definition, "lawbreakers" and "unethical subjects" who are "always already in violation of the law."[34] Creating "laws" and "lawbreakers," the state extends and expands immigration control.[35] The production of "illegality" and the enactment of deportations are yet another form of violation and profound violence in the lives of transnational Mexicans. While the state presumably removes migrants for breaking the law, as discussed in chapter 2, migrants are made "alien" precisely to justify the state's expulsion of so many.

Public discourse focuses on "criminals" who break the law, but the lived experiences of families affected by deportation present alternative moralities. Every migrant I have interviewed, like the vast majority of undocumented migrants in the United States, wants to follow the law; they "really wanna work legal."[36] Transnational Mexicans would willingly take any steps necessary to acquire "legal" status in the United

States, but current immigration laws make a path to legal residence virtually impossible for millions of people living in the country and millions of others outside the nation with ties to those who have already migrated. I have even heard deportees—those who have experienced the ultimate penalty of unauthorized migration and have been formally expelled from the country—express deep respect for the very laws that excluded them.[37]

Throughout my conversations with Federico, he repeatedly spoke of his appreciation of U.S. laws, the laws that were ultimately employed to carry out and justify his removal. As he explained, "In the United States, there is a strong culture of respect for the laws." Attempts to follow the law, such as when Federico applied to change his immigration status through "legal" channels, further complicate this field of morality for transnational migrants. Although public discourse focuses on a simple binary—that is, the notion that people behave in either "legal" or "illegal" ways—the actions and words of migrants raise questions about the stability, and ultimately the morality, of "legality" itself.

And, indeed, lived experience supports the notion that rather than being "felons" or "criminals," deportees are far from the construction that is so easily assigned to them. Although the Obama administration has made it clear that deporting dangerous felons is the priority, the majority of people I spoke with were not felons in any way: they were apprehended or deported explicitly because of their immigration status. Some, such as Emy, were told that they would become felons if they attempted to reenter the country after having been deported for lacking documentation. Others, such as Federico and Gaby, were deported when they tried to secure "legal" status. Still others, such as Rodrigo and Artemio, were deported while following the law, or at least not breaking it. A handful had committed crimes—for example, some had been cited for DWIs, such as Tito's cousin, or driving with open containers of alcohol in a vehicle, as in Jaime's case—but even those acts, as Tito pointed out, would not have carried such life-altering consequences had the individuals been U.S. citizens.

In response to the state's "collection of rules," migrants assert their own "form of action" as "the acceptance or refusal of rules."[38] Within this dialectic, state actions—but also migrants' moralities—"differentiate the permissible from the forbidden [and] . . . what is decent from what is not."[39] Here, the law itself constitutes moralities but not always in expected ways. As Jarrett Zigon outlines, "Perhaps the question should not be whether law and law-like processes are moral or reflect local moral understandings, but instead should ask how law and law-like processes help constitute what counts as the moral . . . for what can justifiably be considered moral."[40] The expression of a divergent moral code also constitutes the in/security of the current moment.

Despite the violations migrants are subject to, migrants themselves understand their transnational movement from a much different perspective, evoking moral codes of their own. For those on the ground, the immorality of laws stems from the production of "illegality." For example, I interviewed Federico in Mexico more than two years after his deportation, yet he continued to be perplexed by a legal system that would expel, in his own words, "good people." Federico asserts counternarratives of morality and immorality when he questions the morality of immigration law: "I'm not saying that it is right [to migrate without authorization], but what about our families? Above all, look at the families, at the people who do not have a bad record, who are not asking for support from the government, who are not committing crimes, nothing like this—but they don't see this. Again and again, we are persecuted because we are Latinos and Mexicans." Here, it is the government that commits immoral acts, through racist action that devalues and divides families.

Transnational Mexicans see themselves as—and nearly always are— ordinary, hardworking people who are committed to their family and children and who, like most of us, will support loved ones at any cost. Instead of an immoral act, they assert undocumented migration as its inverse—something one does for family and children,[41] a supposedly "illegal" act from the perspective of the state, but one that underscores moral responsibility to loved ones, explaining why despite the fact that the state is increasingly "governing immigration through crime,"[42] movement north will and must continue.

As migrants fulfill their responsibility to family and community, they are often caught between these conflicting moral codes: the pervasive legal and social discourse framed in terms of moral and immoral acts, on the one hand, and, on the other, the emic moral codes that guide migration. Migrants perceive their actions as ethical while the state determines that they are breaking the law. Through these alternative moral codes, transmigrants ascribe a kind of morality to "illegality," a purpose to undocumented migration despite its potentially high legal cost. By asserting the "good" in their everyday lives and choices, Mexican migrants challenge constructions of "illegality" and underscore a broader frame of morality that guides migration.

Such alternative moralities describe people who value family and community; who have a strong work ethic and work hard for the nation; who are honest, dependable, and loyal; and who are excluded from formal citizenship despite the many contributions they make, such as taking care of members of the nation by harvesting and preparing food, cleaning homes and workplaces, and watching over the most vulnerable, including young children and the elderly. Migrants' alternative moralities, then, suggest alternative legalities, moral or even "legal" acts that can replace constructions of "illegality." For example, registering one's vehicle or paying the mortgage on time, being a good neighbor or responsible employee, and raising children with strong values—these are actions that migrants believe cannot be dismissed. As Federico told me, "I understand that we, as migrants, made the mistake of crossing the border, but . . . what kind of people are we, bad or good?"

Challenges to the "immoral" aspects of U.S. policies and practices might be read as a form of what the scholar Peter Nyers calls "abject cosmopolitanism," the emergent practices of newcomers through which they contest their exclusion from the nation.[43] If "illegality" is a construction, then there is, perhaps, the potential to change it. Transnational Mexicans counter dehumanizing discourse through their words and through their actions. As Amanda and Tito spoke about lawlessness and the law, they talked about what their family members and law enforcement—and the U.S. government more broadly—should or should not do. They repeated the Spanish word *deber,* which can be used both as a verb, meaning "should," "ought to," or "owe," and as a noun that translates as "debt," "duty," "obligation," or, aptly for labor migrants, "work" or an expected "task." The concept of *deber* connotes an exchange that is profoundly unbalanced. What do migrants owe the nation? What does the nation owe them? How are debts "paid" off, if ever? Are the expectations of undocumented migrants reasonable? Does the "punishment" match the "crime"? During one of our conversations, Jaime posed his own question about this conundrum of im/morality and il/legality: "A lot of people think being an immigrant is a crime, but does it really hurt other people to be an immigrant?"

Deportation results in social disorder, a chaos that migrants describe as uncertainty and unpredictability. Despite the supposed law and order that the state aims to perpetuate through immigration control, state action or inaction leads to insecurity for all members of families within deportation's reach. As the anthropologist Daniel M. Goldstein writes, the law "presents itself as a force of illegality and chaos, rather than of peaceful and equitable ordering," as otherwise law-abiding members of the nation find themselves in the "precarious position . . . of being outlawed."[44] As Mexican nationals are deported and move south, there are many violent settings that they and their loved ones must navigate as states permit or even perpetuate illegal acts.[45] The narratives of transnational Mexicans show how state actions in the name of national security—be it the deportation of migrants or efforts in "the war on drugs"—repeatedly result in insecurity in everyday lives. State efforts to create "security" for some can produce its inverse for others: profound insecurity.

FRAGILITY

As we sat in the courtyard of his mother's home in Mexico, Mauricio tried to make light of the increasing violence there: "I can't believe you are here, with all the insecurity, the violence. I'm very frightened, but look, you and your family—gringos, no less—are here! You seem fine, but see how I am trembling with fear." He dramatically held out a quivering hand, an exaggerated look of terror on his face. But while Mauricio joked about the changes in Mexico, the gravity of the situation was clear. Even as we laughed at his performance, everyone knew that the violence was indeed widespread if not inescapable.

Mauricio and his brother, Hugo, made the trip from the United States to visit their mother and to celebrate Mother's Day with her. Both men had married U.S. citizens and naturalized as U.S. citizens themselves years earlier, so movement back and forth was much easier for them than it was for family members without documents. With their U.S. passports, they could travel north and south across the U.S.-Mexico border more frequently than family and friends and in ways that many could not. Still, this return was a reluctant one. The men told me that they had been hesitant to make the trip, but because it was important to celebrate with their aging mother, they decided that it was worth the risk. Their wives were scared to see them go but agreed that honoring their mother should be a priority. While Hugo and Mauricio had typically traveled by car to Mexico, accompanied by their wives and children, they knew that this time, as migrants driving a shiny new SUV, they would be targets for carjackings, kidnappings, or worse. So for this trip they had opted to return by bus, without other family members.

As Hugo and Mauricio talked of the alternative arrangements they had made to cross from north to south, there were parallels with other forms of transnational movement. Like migrations north, the border crossing was shaped by aspects of one's positionality, including gender, age, family position, and national membership.[46] And while U.S. citizenship can facilitate migration, it is not necessarily a guarantee of safe passage. The very economic prosperity and legal citizenship that are the goals of many migrants who travel north were precisely the things that made Hugo and Mauricio's travel south insecure. Movement therefore can be perilous for all transnational Mexicans. While different statuses and circumstances create particular risks, forms, and settings of violence confronting individuals and their families, there are also continuities that can be traced across borders and throughout communities in this age of deportation. A seemingly casual and celebratory Mother's Day trip—taken by some but not possible for others—brings into relief how violence divides families and directs, forces, limits, and/or prevents various forms of return despite the formal status of the travelers.

So how does one manage such insecurity in everyday exchanges? What happens when individuals and families return or are forcibly returned to places that are plagued by violence and uncertainty? And how can migrants navigate the insecurities they face in the United States? For many transnational Mexicans, the response to multiple forms of violence involves the search for security in its absence. Throughout my research, transnational Mexicans described "just trying to survive." Survival often means waiting—waiting for U.S. immigration reform, waiting for a political solution to end drug violence, waiting for a future characterized by tranquillity. Narratives of survival demonstrate how, in addition to the transnational geographies of violence, expressions of insecurity also circulate along temporal scales as lives and acts are deferred to safer, more certain times. Temporality shapes such discourse, as migrants reference memories of the past to convey hopes for an alternative future. Movement through time and memory, and across distance, characterizes the insecurity—and fragility—of the current moment.

. . .

After a bomb threat at a private school run by an order of nuns in the city of Zacatecas, I spoke with the school's director. The school served children of all ages, from preschoolers to high school students, and the fact that such young children had been the target of the threat was very unsettling in the community. The director explained that school administrators were working with authorities to ensure a swift investigation and that the police were checking phone records in an attempt to track down the caller. At first, the director speculated that perhaps the threat had come from an older student who was trying to avoid an exam. She quickly dismissed that possibility, however, saying that the threat had probably come from "*los malos*," the people I had so often heard referred to and whose aim it seemed was to create unease in the community. "Yes," she said, as she thought about it more, "bad people" seemed the most likely culprits since there had been several threats around town that same week, at schools and public buildings, including a childcare facility for infants and toddlers.

What, I wondered aloud, would cause individuals to make such threats? Here, the director talked about violence in a broader context—much like Johan Galtung's concept of "structural violence"[47]—situating it within a transnational space. She explained that this was a difficult time, economically and socially, in both Mexico and the United States, and that it was important to remember that such violence is, above all, linked to poverty and social suffering. As she stated emphatically, echoing what I had heard from so many: "People are just trying to survive." She spoke of a common "humanity," connecting the struggles that people currently face in Mexico to the experiences of Mexicans living in the United States. She again deployed the language of survival in her description of how she understands the drug trade and labor migrations to be intertwined: "There are some people in the drug trade, some *narcos,* who are involved because they are 'bad,' but there are many who are desperate, who are just trying to survive." In the end, both migrating to the United States and involvement in the drug economy in Mexico are strategies aimed at getting by.

The school director's perspective reminded me of a conversation I had had with Dina and her husband, Sergio, as we discussed insecurity in Mexico and the United States. They had similarly described desperate and intersecting economic and social conditions, and they, too, like many of the individuals I talked with, used the verb *sobrevivir* (to survive) as they spoke of the multiple insecurities they faced: financial hardship, the difficulties of living in the United States without papers, growing violence in Mexico. These geographically distant and seemingly distinct conditions and experiences converge for transnational Mexicans, who must do complex calculations of risk in order to survive. After two years of working in the north, Sergio was now living in Mexico again. Although the decision to return from the United States and its promise of—or at least potential for—financial security was a difficult one, both Sergio and Dina felt it was for the best. Leaving behind stable work in a community with an increasing number of deportations, Sergio had been reluctant to return to Mexico—much like Mauricio and Hugo—but it seemed the better option when faced with insecurity in two places. The couple recounted how, as they weighed the possibility of living apart, with Sergio in the United States, or reuniting back in Mexico, the options did not seem very different in the end. As Dina described it, "Here or there, it's the same . . . surviving, it's what we do—so better that we are together here, right?"

Always somewhat unpredictable, transnational movement in an age of deportation is even more so, as the conditions under which migration and return occur are increasingly uncertain. Transnational subjects continue to cross borders north and south, but the insecurity of "lawlessness" and "the law," the transnational circulation of violence, and the narratives of im/morality that shape interactions between the state and individuals mean that returns in either direction are often reluctant ones. Migrants come and go, stay and leave, arrive and depart amid violence and expanding U.S. immigration control. After the bomb threat at the school in Zacatecas, one mother asked, "But what can we do? Where is it safe?" After the incident in the town plaza, several people left the area, including the town's priest, although this was not an option for most residents. As Dina recounted the terrifying details of the event, she ended our conversation with a similar sentiment: "We are all very fearful of the violence, but where can we go? Where would it be any different?"

In my exchanges with transnational Mexicans, a kind of hopelessness has framed discussions about the future. The social ills that extend transnationally register as collective trauma, evoking survival responses among families and within communities. The questions of transnational Mexicans—"What can we do?," "Where can we go?"—are not easily answered since the migration that may have once seemed a solution accompanied by measurable risks has evolved into more danger and violation. As violence circulates transnationally, some lives are more at risk than others. The fragility of everyday life can be plotted structurally, among the barely visible and rarely viable strategies for survival that transnational subjects can access. *Inseguridad* grows as migrants look for a way out of threatening environments that move ever closer to home.

CHAPTER 4

Fragmentation

Everything falls apart when you get deported.

—Jaime

As Federico described the fallout of deportation, he emphasized pain and family separation: "It hurts us to be apart." He referred to the trial that had ended in removal orders for both him and his wife, Gaby, the only undocumented migrants in the family. Federico focused on how deportation had divided kin: "The judge didn't understand what family means to us . . . he did the opposite." The judge's decision inverted not only Federico's logic, but his life: in deportation's aftermath, his familiar world turned upside down. Dispossessed of kinship as it once was, he and his loved ones were forced to reconfigure family life across geographic and time differences—literally, across long distances and time zones but also in the temporal negotiations of actions delayed to an uncertain future when they might be together again in one place. Earlier, I described the irony that "home" was taken away precisely as and because Federico and Gaby attempted formally to claim membership through legal channels. Following the deportation, the family was divided by a border, despite the U.S. citizenship of five of the seven family members. Federico and Gaby and their children were dispossessed of home, nation, membership, and future.

Initially, the family went south together to Mexico: Federico and Gaby went back to their home community in rural Zacatecas, and their five children paradoxically "returned" to Mexico for the first time. After the family spent a few weeks in their new home, the two eldest children went back to the United States, twenty-four-year-old Leo to continue his studies and twenty-one-year-old Clara, expecting a baby, to reunite with her husband. Where precisely "family" was to reside was a challenge. Clara had immediate family members in two countries. Leo was faced with a difficult choice: dispossession of home and the future he had imagined in the United States or dispossession of daily life with loved ones. Federico and Gaby, wanting the best possible educational and employment opportunities for all of their children, encouraged Leo and Clara to go north, so they returned once again, this time to the United States.

For a period, the family lived split in this transnational configuration: two adult children, a son-in-law, and a newborn grandson living north of the border and the parents and three children in Mexico. Federico and Gaby and their younger children—Naty, Mia, and Ana, ages 18, 17, and 10—continued to live in Mexico following deportation and tried to build new lives there; meanwhile, Leo and Clara aimed to reconstruct and reconfigure lives in the United States. Because of Federico and Gaby's undocumented status in the United States, the children who stayed with them had never been to their parents' hometown, so it was, as the teenage daughters made clear when they spoke with me about it, quite an adjustment. Yet they were also respectful of the bind the family was in and the difficult decision their parents had made, first to embark on an uncertain life in the United States and later to bring them "back" to Mexico. Federico and Gaby felt it was especially important to have the youngest children, all girls, with them. The three went to school, but, Federico said, the abrupt shift in their studies posed difficulties. The family did the best they could to manage the challenges and to adjust to an unknown future path.

A year after their "return" to Mexico, the geographies of family again changed. First, Naty wed, and she and her new husband went north, joining an uncle and several cousins in Colorado. Soon after, Mia also returned to the United States and enrolled in a local community college. The family still lived divided by the U.S.-Mexico border but in a new way. Most family members were in the United States—four of the five children—while Federico and Gaby and their youngest daughter, Ana, remained in Mexico. Although transnational and mixed-status families are typically divided by migration, theirs is a family fragmented and specifically reconfigured because of deportation.

DISPOSSESSION

As Federico and Gaby and their children experienced firsthand, the deportation of Mexican nationals has a profound effect on kin relations and is resulting in new, emergent forms of transnational and mixed-status families. Analysis of the actions of family members and kin groups yields a route to understanding how the disorder of state action plays out, at times unpredictably, in the most intimate settings. In turn, it is possible to further interrogate and to begin to catalog the chaos of removal and return. When families are faced with the deportation of loved ones, they are soon situated within fragmented geographies and disrupted futures, often along gendered lines. Im/mobilities and discombobulated scales of time upset family life, as kin groups aim to re/locate family members and plan for futures that will foster well-being and stability—a daunting task when confronted by transnational violence and the disorder of deportation.

I use the concept *dispossession* in order to trace these forms of suffering that reconfigure gendered familial relations after deportation. As Judith Butler and Athena Athanasiou posit, dispossession "implies imposed injuries, painful interpellations, occlusions, and foreclosures."[1] This is dispossession as "expulsion,"[2] for there is a notable difference between "'being' dispossessed, on the one side, and 'becoming' or 'being made' dispossessed, on the other."[3] Dispossession cultivates precarity—as "vulnerability to injury and loss"—but is also a form of "precaritization,"[4] the process through which one is made precarious by others. Explicitly through state action, individuals and their families are dispossessed not only of material possessions but also of less quantifiable, more abstract things, including home, nation, and relationships with one another. As the state expels migrants from the country through removal, family life and family ties become ever more precarious despite families' resistance to these violent ruptures.

The dispossession that families experience plays out as fragmentation along both spatial and temporal scales. Families face dispossession of home, as familial geographies are characterized by new configurations of separation. Similarly, the dispossession of time interrupts plans and trajectories among kin networks. In addition, dispossession has gendered dimensions that develop as deportation both follows and challenges patterns that have formed through migrations over generations and across long distances. Here, I trace the ruptures of gendered kin ties through the dispossession of place, as both home and nation, and the dispossession of time, as families witness a brutal taking away of what once was and, significantly, what could have been.

Transnational families are very familiar with lives "divided by borders"[5] and increasingly "scattered"[6] because of global movement. Given that transnational experience shapes and even defines the networks of so many, what is different about family separation caused by deportation rather than migration? As illustrated in previous chapters, when the U.S. state removes a family member, families are upended as they scramble to make arrangements to ensure the safety of children and reconnect partners, parents and children, and siblings as they are able. On the one hand, the reconfigurations of family that follow a deportation can parallel those that are the result of migration. On the other hand, because the impetus and processes of deportation are distinct from other forms of migration, the reconfigurations engendered by deportation are unprecedented.

Whereas the placements of family members in either nation through migration are often made after months or even years of planning, the locations of individuals after removal must most often be pulled together on a truncated timeline amid chaos and crisis. If young children are involved, the stakes are even higher, as families scramble to reunite partners, arrange residences in one country or the other for their members, and ensure care for children in a transnational space. Transnational Mexicans find that the separation of deportation can come to define family relations. Family that extends across long distances also occurs because of immigration, but deportability and deportation intensify the divides, often because they are considered final or irreversible. Indeed, because of deportation, a family may be permanently altered.

As family members are separated from and dispossessed of home and national membership, they engage in novel arrangements and alternative imaginings of kin relations. As part of the restructuring of family that occurs due to the direction and disruption of migration flows caused by deportation, gender roles, too, may be troubled or redefined. These forcible redefinitions result in new configurations of transnational partnerships and relations along the geographic and temporal lines discussed above. When families and couples are fragmented—separated across space and time—they are dispossessed of meaningful places, of social context, of a rooted historical tie to place, of access to their past lives, and of aspirations for the future.

Family Geographies

During a visit with Emy shortly after she returned to Mexico, I was surprised to hear a conversation in English coming from the next room. "Do you have visitors from the United States?," I asked. "No, those are my children!," she laughed, and called for them to join us in the living room. "My four children are here with me now. It's most difficult for the oldest ones. They all miss their father, of course, but for Cora and Joaquín it has been especially challenging." The children had only been with Emy a short time when we spoke, so the move to Mexico and all of its stresses were still fresh. She described how painful it was to have the family living apart, with Emy and the children in Mexico and Emy's husband, Manuel, in the United States. Emy was not sure what would happen next, so she tried to focus on the present: getting the kids enrolled in school and helping them adjust to a new place.

Prior to the deportation, Emy and Manuel had lived in the United States for extended periods without documents, migrating between the two countries for years at a time. Their four children are U.S. citizens. Recall that Emy's parents and brother were tragically killed in an automobile accident, prompting her return to Mexico. It was when she attempted to return "home" to the United States that she was deported. Immediately after the deportation, the family was in crisis. They struggled to make a plan for how and where they would reunite, which family members would live together, and how residence across a transnational space would be structured. Emy and Manuel first made the decision to have the children stay in the United States with Manuel; later, after the challenges Manuel faced juggling full-time work and parenting, they decided that the children should join Emy in Mexico. Still, Emy told me, even though she was reunited with the children, nothing was yet settled; in fact, everything felt uncertain. She explained that during the upcoming year they would consider what was best for the family and make plans accordingly.

The geographic dis/placements of family after deportation are multiple. At different junctures, Emy and her family and Federico and Gaby and their children embarked on new arrangements of family life; kinship was structured transnationally but also split by the U.S.-Mexico border. Within intimate spheres, these geographies of return are fragmented, as individuals are forced to move, move with others, do not move, or cannot move when they wish to. This is a form of forced transnationalism and disruptions of time—certainly for those deported but also for loved ones connected to them. Deportation is situated within transnational movement more broadly, as the directionality and destinations of migration and return shift and are reconfigured.

For those affected by removal, the geographies of deportation are complicated and can be chaotic, characterized by mobility *and* immobility, as individual family members are caught in either nation, resulting in both new and familiar forms of divided transnational kin networks. Even as deportation is itself movement across borders, state removals also result in limited, restricted, or even completely prohibited movement, with people trapped in a particular nation. This tension, too, is part of the chaos and unpredictability related to return. Shifts in the geographies of family produce changes in nearly every aspect of family life, from daily, mundane acts to larger, long-term plans that kin groups must make within the constraints of deportation.

Emy and her family, for example, experienced different mobilities after deportation, beginning with Emy's forced movement. Emy was detained while attempting to enter the United States and then forcibly moved by U.S. agents into the United States, only to move again, as she was formally removed from the country. This is undeniably forced migration, first north and then south, as Emy was moved spatially by state agents through detention and removal. Through return, lives are uprooted: people are in one geographic place leading a particular life, and then within a relatively short period they may be relocated, forced to live elsewhere.

Emy's forced migrations, orchestrated by the state, produced a series of other forms of movement, especially the migrations of her children. These are mobilities that are controlled and designed, directly and indirectly, by the state. Family networks are both *de*territorialized and *re*territorialized as the result of U.S. state actions.[7] When Emy was deported, for example, the family was deterritorialized as Emy was— from the U.S. government's perspective at least—permanently displaced from her family's home. Next, Emy and Manuel made arrangements for the children to migrate to Mexico to be reunited with Emy, as they were reterritorialized, with Manuel in the United States and Emy and the children in Mexico.

Deportation's migrations signal a shift in unanticipated directionalities as people are increasingly moving from north to south rather than south to north, as with previous migration flows from Mexico. Similarly, the transborder movement of Federico's family resulted in deterritorialized, then reterritorialized family and disrupted assumptions about directionality, as all family members initially migrated from north to south, leaving no one in the United States despite the U.S. citizenship of five of the seven family members. In addition, the deportations of Federico and Gaby created new migrations as their children went to Mexico for the first time and then the two eldest children returned to California, "migrating" north through an emergent kind of return migration, leaving family behind to pursue opportunities in the United States.

Immobility, too, accompanies or even defines deportation. Paradoxically, movement can entail no actual movement or even entrapment, as the ability to cross borders is closely controlled by the state. For Emy and her loved ones, deportation was characterized by such immobility as she found herself stuck or caught, first in a federal detention center in Texas. After the removal, she was again caught, this time in her home nation, Mexico. And just as Emy was trapped in Mexico, her husband, Manuel, was trapped in the United States, unable to migrate south if he was to continue as his family's primary breadwinner.

As Emy discussed arrangements the family might make—that is, to have Emy "return" to the United States or to have Manuel come back to Mexico—she expressed the profound uncertainty they faced. Just as Emy and Manuel were trapped on opposite sides of the U.S.-Mexico border, their U.S. citizen children found themselves living in a country that was not their own, also "trapped" until the family made other arrangements or until they were old enough to migrate without caregivers. Because of their U.S. citizenship, the children, in principle at least, could move, but in all practical senses they were confined to Mexico until their parents could make arrangements for an alternative residence.

During our many conversations, it was clear that the deportation had interrupted family life, perhaps indefinitely. Even as Emy suggested that return migration to the United States might be a possibility, albeit an increasingly difficult one, she felt defeated and quite tentative about what the future held for her and her family. Prior to the deportation, Emy had migrated multiple times between the United States and Mexico—an unusual migration history for a young woman but one that reflected her independence and tenacity. Confident and with a keen sense of humor, Emy had struck me as almost invincible. Not in this case, however. She was withdrawn and quieter than usual; she told me she cried often and felt hopeless about what was next.

One day as we talked about the implications of the deportation, Emy commented, "You can go and come, but we can't." Indeed, rather than an inalienable right, the freedom of movement is always determined by one's national membership,[8] but it is also embedded in relatedness to others. Again and again, as Emy recounted the removal, she articulated the sense and reality of being trapped during detention and in her daily life following the deportation. As the transnational geographies of return make clear, the spatial dimensions of kinship after deportation include both movement and barriers to it, as individuals and families find themselves unpredictably migrating in unexpected directions and to new destinations but also forced or unable to do so.

Temporalities of Kin

For Carlos—husband, father of six, and primary wage earner— deportation profoundly disrupted family life. Carlos's deportation, and the kind of time travel it produced, was enmeshed with kin ties and the trajectories of his wife and children. I described how Carlos had been deported after a series of border crossings following the death of his father. Like Emy, a family crisis had been the impetus for Carlos's unexpected return to Mexico. Despite his undocumented status and the serious risk inherent in attempted reentry into the United States, he made the difficult decision to go to Mexico precisely because of family obligations. And, also like Emy, Carlos was deported when he had attempted to "go back" north, leaving some family members behind in Mexico to reunite with other family members in the United States.

For Carlos and his family, life was upended after the deportation, and future imaginings were suddenly halted. The "return" of family members from the United States to Mexico followed a trajectory similar to their migrations over the years but in a more condensed time period. Over a span of two years, the family migrated "back" to Mexico in stages or steps. First, after Carlos was released from U.S. immigration detention, he went to the rancho and lived by himself for several months. Recall that it was when he started drinking and suggested he might sell the family farm that Lucía made the decision to go back to Mexico with their two school-aged children.

Meanwhile, several family members remained in Texas. Three adult children and Marisol, a junior in high school at the time—all of whom had been living without documents in the United States for most of their lives—decided to stay. Two of these adult children were married, with U.S. citizen children of their own, so their ties to the nation, despite the lack of formal membership, were strong. After Marisol graduated from high school her parents made arrangements for her to return to Mexico, leaving the three eldest children living in Dallas with their spouses and children. Even after multiple migrations and configurations of residence at different stages and moments in time the family remains apart.

The temporalities of deportation involve going back—spatially and through time. In addition, deportation renders lives frozen in the moment.

Finally, and perhaps most troubling for deportees and their loved ones, forced removal frames the future as an unimaginable, even interminable, passage of time. Whereas migration focuses on the future and is typically driven by hope and perceived opportunities, deportation and return migration result in its inverse: despair and the narrowing of possible trajectories. Again and again, the temporal im/mobilities of deportation reshape family life.

The experiences of Carlos and his family demonstrate this movement through time. When Carlos went "back" to Mexico, he also went back in time. After making the United States his home for more than a decade, he found himself living in the past, with no promise for the future. During his first weeks back in Mexico, Carlos was initially hopeful. He thought he could resume his life from before, and in some ways he did: he reconnected with family and friends, and he made plans to farm on his land once more. But Carlos had gone back to a past that was no longer there: his father was gone, his mother's health was deteriorating, his siblings' families were divided by migration.

Prior to the deportation, Carlos and his family had experienced a form of chain migration across space and time. In the 1990s, Carlos had migrated to the United States to work and send money back to his family in Mexico. After several years apart, Carlos's wife, Lucía, and their five children—who at the time ranged in age from two to thirteen—went north to "reunite" with Carlos. The family then lived together in Texas for nearly fifteen years, during which time another child, Nico, was born. Their lives became rooted in the United States: the children attended school, Carlos had dependable work, and Lucía made friends and started a small catering business.

Like the chain migration that had reunited the family years before in the United States, a kind of *chain return* involved geographic and temporal shifts. Yet, while the family's migration north was forward-focused, their return was discombobulating: time was mixed up. Carlos and Lucía went to a place where time had moved ahead without them. For the children, return meant going to a time from the past that they had never known. Since Nico is a U.S. citizen, he had never been to Mexico until his father was deported. The other children had few or no memories of Mexico and had lives built in the United States. Two adult children had partners and their own children, which tethered them to the United States despite their undocumented status. For all family members, the deportation launched a foreign life and an unknown future.

Similarly, Federico and his family moved through unexpected time dimensions. Initially, they planned for the future by applying for residency. When Federico learned from an attorney that he was eligible to apply for permanent residency, he was elated. But when they received word from USCIS that the process was not likely to work out as they thought it would, they were compelled to revisit their initial migration decades earlier and the events that had led them to come to the United States in the first place. Finally, they were shocked by the suddenness of the deportation order, which moved them rapidly toward an uncertain trajectory.

For Federico and Gaby and their children, return to Mexico was both a reversal and a new trajectory. Futures were recast as they struggled to define an unexpected life in Mexico, for themselves, but also for their U.S. citizen children. Even though four of their five children eventually went back in the United States after varying lengths of time in Mexico, future plans for all family members required a recalibration of time. With no possible authorized return on the horizon for Federico and Gaby, each family member was forced to rethink place of residence and ties to—and distance from—two nations, individually and as a collective. Family reunification through time and space—and this unpredictability of location and future imaginings—can come to frame daily life for *all* family members, regardless of each person's national membership or place of residence.

These are disrupted families and interrupted futures. Emy told me that she and her children were "losing time" while in Mexico. Carlos and Lucía speculated often about what the future held for them; after making the United States home for more than a decade, they found themselves living in the past, with little promise for the future. Federico researched pardons and possible legal options that might one day reunite his family in the United States, but attorneys told him the chances were slim. Geographies and temporalities intersect as individuals and families reinvent their futures in the aftermath of deportation. Removal produces a convergence of temporal scales, a collapsing and/or interdependence of past, present, and future. This is dispossession as disruption, as the deportation of a family member means that time together is taken away, for a period or indefinitely.

GENDERED FRAGMENTATION

In chapter 1 I recounted Mariela's description of the changes that were taking place in her small town because of deportation. She had rattled off the names of the many men who had recently been deported. The list grew, and then she paused. "Oh, and also Emy." Surprised, I asked, "Emy is the only woman?" "Yes," Mariela confirmed, "and now she is here in the rancho alone." As Mariela described Emy's deportation, she used the word *sola* in two senses: only and alone. This notion of *sola/o*—as alone but also as exception—is a way to consider the gendered fragmentation caused by deportation. I have outlined how families are divided across time and space, but these fractures in kin relations also occur according to gendered patterns. Indeed, deportation is shaping the trajectories of transnational subjects and their families in particularly gendered ways.

Part of the reason that Emy is understood to be *sola,* as exception, is the context in which migrants are being deported: the region where I have conducted fieldwork in Mexico has a long history of gendered migrations—and specifically masculinized migrations—that continue to shape current movements north. In previous research, I focused on these gendered aspects of migration.[9] People have repeatedly spoken of "*los que se van* [the men who go]" and "*las que se quedan* [the women who stay]."[10] Current migrations from the region where Mariela and Emy live are, like previous migrations, masculinized and primarily controlled by men: men usually go north to work, and women typically migrate with or to join a male partner or other relatives. The autonomous movement and migration of women is much more regulated than that of males and, in general, is actively discouraged by families and communities, who perceive movement by women as some combination of risky and unseemly. Often, too, women are expected to be the primary caregivers of children, so they are more likely to "stay" in Mexico with young family members. Masculinized migrations result in transnational households in which men are concentrated in the United States and women and children in towns in Mexico. Although there are exceptions—such as men who do not migrate or women who migrate independently—the gendered dimensions of migration persist.

Removal and return are similarly experienced in uniquely gendered ways. As a result of increased deportations, reverse migrations are increasingly common for females as well as males. The expulsion by the U.S. state of primarily male migrants is what the sociologists Tanya Golash-Boza and Pierrette Hondagneu-Sotelo call "gendered racial removal,"[11] statistically and experientially. I saw similar gendered patterns in my research, as men were most frequently those who were deported and women were again "left behind"—in this case, increasingly in the United States—or followed partners to new or previous destinations. The term "left behind" has been employed by scholars to describe those who stay in home communities while others migrate. Although it is a problematic term,[12] it does have resonance in the case of deportation because women and children are likely to stay where they are, for a period at least, when men are deported.

In the few cases when married women or women in partnerships are deported *sola*, gender relations also shift, as the care of children and future roles are renegotiated. Children may remain in the United States with a father or older sibling who has not been deported, or they may "return" to Mexico with a mother who now must care for them on her own. Furthermore, after deportation women may embark on autonomous migrations for the first time as men stay or are potentially "left behind" through yet another inversion of deportation and its familiar narratives. I propose extending literature on gender and migration to consider the specifically gendered dimensions of return:[13] what does it mean for gender relations and subjectivities when movement shifts directions, when migrations are also "returns"?

Sola/o

One morning when I tapped on Emy's gate with a coin, it took a minute for her to answer. When she came to the door she seemed very upset and disoriented. She was wiping tears from her eyes. "Excuse me, I've been crying," she said. "My uncle and I were talking about my mother, my father, my brother . . . there has been such sadness, such loss." "*Estoy tan sola* [I am so lonely (or alone)]," she continued, her eyes again tearing up. "I miss my family so . . . I keep thinking I am going to see them. I'm in the kitchen, and I think one of them walks by in another room. It is so difficult to be here alone [*sola*] in the house without them." It was the tragic death of Emy's parents and brother that had prompted her return to the rancho a year earlier, a trip that eventually had culminated with her deportation. Now, back in Mexico again, Emy felt lonely and very much alone, even when she was with other people in the community.

After deportation a woman is likely to find herself *sola* in the sense of being alone or by herself but also *sola* as exception. Each time I talked with Emy about the deportation, she repeatedly referred to herself as *sola* in these different senses. She was one of the few women in the community to migrate north alone, one of even fewer to be detained and deported, and the only woman I interviewed who was deported "alone," or without her husband. Emy's nearly fifteen years of migrations between Mexico and the United States prior to the deportation had not been typical for a woman: she first migrated autonomously as a young newlywed in order to reunite with her first husband. She told me that she could not tolerate being alone without him in the rancho, so she crossed the border again alone, and went to San Diego, California, and began working. When the marriage dissolved, she spent time alone once more, now in the United States. Eventually, she brought her U.S. citizen children to her hometown and then migrated several times on her own while her children stayed with relatives in Mexico. Years later, she remarried after meeting Manuel in a neighboring town.

Emy thus repeatedly crossed the border and was deported, *sola*. Back in Mexico, she recounted the difficulties of wading through uncommon and unknown territory. She is again without her husband, raising her children and looking forward to the day when she will be reunited with him, in the rancho or perhaps, she tells me, in the United States. As the only woman deportee living in her town without her spouse, she is indeed *sola* in both senses of the word, an exception to gendered patterns of deportation and also lonely and living without the daily support of her husband.

In one of deportation's many reversals, Emy's husband, Manuel, similarly spent time alone, or in his case *solo,* during the detention and deportation, although he was in the United States. For several months Manuel cared for the children "on his own" while working full-time. Then, after the children returned, Manuel lived *solo* in the United States. Manuel and Emy currently live apart; both are alone as they plan for a future together as best they can. Emy told me that she and Manuel were unwilling to live in different countries long-term: "My husband wants me to go there, or for him to come here. He says he doesn't want to continue to be alone.

"Left Behind"

Like Emy, Lucía described the many ways that she is *sola:* "Here in Mexico, I'm always alone . . . I don't ever go out, I'm always here in my house alone. Look how my life has changed." But unlike Emy, Lucía's loneliness occurs despite the fact that she is currently living with her husband in Mexico. Lucía feels alone because of her husband's deportation, even though she is not currently separated from him. For Lucía, being *sola* also meant being "left alone" for a stretch or, as it is framed in the migration literature, "left behind." When Carlos was deported and returned to Mexico, Lucía initially stayed in Dallas with their six children. She continued working there, "left behind" in the United States after already having spent many years "left behind" in Mexico while her husband worked in Dallas. Because of Carlos's deportation, she was "left behind" once more, this time in Texas.

Lucía spent nearly a year alone in the United States, first while Carlos traveled to be with his family after his father's death and then during and after Carlos's detention and deportation. So, Lucía was *sola* for nearly a year before the family reunited in Mexico. Now, in the rancho, Lucía laments her husband's deportation and her own return. She told me that life has been difficult since the deportation and her resulting migration to Mexico. She recounted that she and Carlos argue often, that they never have money even for the basics, that the children are having difficulty in school, and that she misses her children in the United States. In a time of record deportations, the locations and positions of migrants are shifting and inverting: those "left behind" are increasingly living in *el norte* rather than "at home" in Mexico. Due to the history of masculinized migration from many parts of Mexico, this sentiment of "*las que se quedan*"—regardless of whether it is in Mexico or the United States—is familiar: women know well what it means to be alone, as well as the struggles and potential (albeit limited) opportunities it brings.

As the experiences of these two couples—Lucía and Carlos and Emy and Manuel—demonstrate, men can also find themselves on their own, *solo* or left behind in either country. Carlos had migrated alone to the United States decades earlier, and his deportation meant that he also spent an unexpected and extended period alone in Mexico. Manuel, who previously had migrated to the United States while Emy was left behind in Mexico for a period, was in the unusual position of being the one left behind when Emy was deported, this time in the United States. Given the recent increase in deportations, "*los que se van*" are increasingly "*los que regresan*" (the men who return) or even the men "left behind" in unpredictable geographic locations. Finally, as the risk of deportation increases and job opportunities decrease in the United States, the gendered politics of going and staying are often mixed up. It is likely that the number of *los que se quedan* will grow as fewer men make the trip north in the first place.

Gendered Returns

When Antonia's husband returned after six years in the United States, she told me, her life again, like when her partner first migrated, changed significantly: "*Ya no estoy sola* [Now I am not alone] . . . now my husband is here." When I initially met Antonia years earlier, her husband was in the United States, and we spent much of our time socializing together and with others. When I visited with her after her husband's return, however, her demeanor and our interactions were markedly different. As we talked and caught up, her husband was replacing a tire on their truck, just feet from us. His presence was strong and palpable; Antonia hardly spoke, and after a few minutes she excused herself to get dinner started; she said that she was sorry but she could not talk for long. As she walked into the house and I went toward the gate to leave, she quickly looked back and waved before disappearing into the kitchen. In this case, the return of Antonia's partner meant the return of Antonia to a less independent state. If in many cases the disruption and redrawing of family relations is seen as a negative condition in which previously united families undergo forcible divisions, Antonia's case shows that, for some, deportation and the gendering of its accompanying chaos can create new roles. In this case, a necessarily *sola* and independent Antonia who stayed in Mexico finds herself negotiating a more proscriptive role since she and her husband were reunited.

I have focused here on the ways that migrants are "alone" or "left behind" as a result of deportation, but there is another emergent process that will be important to trace in the years to come. Today, with men returning to Mexico because of deportation, as well as the economic crisis and limited job opportunities in the north, there are additional shifts in previous gendered patterns of transnational movement: small ranchos throughout the region—known previously as places of "all" or "only" women[14]—are seeing changes in their gendered composition. Many of the women I interviewed who were without spouses a decade ago are once again living with their husbands, "reunited" in Mexico rather than in the United States as they had once hoped. And although a reunion with a partner after years apart can be emotionally rewarding, women I spoke with communicated ambivalence about the return of a partner and the subsequent changes in the levels of agency they experienced. Women said that their day-to-day lives may improve, but there is also an attendant loss of independence when a partner is at home once more.

This trend reveals that in many ways women are again—or still—disadvantaged within the gender politics of transnationality. These are what Sarah Mahler and Patricia Pessar have called "gendered geographies of power,"[15] but with specifics that are both parallel to and different from the experience of masculinized migration that has shaped movement for decades. As times change, there are likely to be emergent patterns of feminized migrations: as more men are forced to return to Mexico, women who once stayed while partners went may become "*las que se van,*" or the women who go, migrating autonomously, whether north or south, in response to deportation. It is likely that whether migrants go alone or stay alone—or are reunited with a partner—a persistent frame of gendered and specifically male power will direct who moves and who stays, even as women act in spheres that are newly available to them.

As the migrations and deportations of women and men take these new forms, migrants are increasingly or still *sola/o*—alone and on their own. During my ongoing conversations with Lucía and Emy, they continued to evoke the sentiment of being *sola*. Lucía told me she would go to the United States on her own if her husband permitted it, while Emy said she would have to stay in the rancho alone until she and her husband could make other plans. Emy was emphatic that neither she nor Manuel wanted to continue to live alone, that it simply was not sustainable: "If we make it across the border, we will do it together, and if we are not able to cross, we will not cross together. If we can't get into the United States, we will stay here, together."

FAMILY DEUNIFICATION

Earlier, I introduced Jaime, who was deported when he was a teenager. During Jaime's immigration hearing, the judge asked if he had any family members who were from the United States. Feeling hopeful, Jaime mentioned his two siblings who are U.S. citizens. "No," the judge clarified, "do you have any *immediate* family members who are U.S. citizens?" Jaime recounted being confused by this question. To his mind, of course his siblings were part of his immediate family. But the judge explained that by "immediate family members," he meant parents, children, or a spouse. Jaime was surprised by the speed of the process and especially of this discussion of one's "family," given the significance of family to him personally: "The judge just reads you your rights, and then he asks, 'Are you married to a citizen?' No. 'Do you have any citizen

non cohesive story—telling pieces and parts

kids?' No. 'Are your parents citizens?' I said, 'No.' 'Well, then,' said the judge. 'I can't do anything for you. You have to leave.' And that's it." Jaime said that people who did have U.S. citizen family members—the "right" family members—were assigned another court date, and the people who did not, "Well, that's it."

All of Jaime's immediate family—those he and the state define as such—lived in the United States at the time of his deportation; some were recognized as formal members of the nation, and others were not. Still, these different configurations of family relations and formal membership were not sufficient to justify a "deferral of removal" for Jaime from the perspective of the state. His U.S. citizen siblings did not "count" as family, and his undocumented migrant parents, despite living in the United States for decades, were not considered members of the nation. The government narrowly defined both "family" and "membership" in ways that excluded significant family members *and* U.S. citizens—legal and de facto—from consideration. Jaime was forcibly disconnected from the many loved ones who lived in and contributed to the United States. He said it was as if he "didn't matter" because of the immigration status of those he loved. He was silent for a moment as he recalled that painful day in court, and then he summed up the proceedings: "You matter if you are married to a citizen or have a citizen kid or if your parents are citizens. That's all. If you don't have any of the three, you can't stay. You gotta leave."

For those who are deported, such as Federico, Carlos, Emy, and, significantly, the circles of kin around them, family ties did indeed—in Jaime's words—"fall apart." After deportation, families are fragmented across space, people are forced to "disappear" from family life, and the temporalities of kin trajectories are disrupted. Analysis that pays close attention to time, place, and gender reveals families divided; the dispossession of home and imagined futures; separation from loved ones; places of residence that cannot be accessed or inhabited; intimate relationships that are reconfigured; moments with family that will never come; generations of kin that may no longer be. Yet, while Jaime describes a set of circumstances without assigning agency, in each of these cases family life was, in fact, *taken* apart. The fragmentation, disruption, separation, and dispossession caused by deportation can be traced to direct acts and intention: these are families "undone" by state policies and actions.[16]

Indeed, in circumstances of deportation, kinship is not a "fully autonomous sphere, proclaimed to be distinct from . . . the regulations of the state."[17] State regimes permeate family relations and restructure kinship. U.S. immigration policies are ostensibly designed to facilitate family reunification but can have contradictory effects within migrant families.[18] Deportation results in reunification's certain inverse: a form of *family deunification*. Such deunification, brought on by state action—increased deportations, deportability, border controls, policing, and more—is the antithesis of family reunited, disrupting and even dismantling transnational families, separating and displacing members of kin networks throughout Mexico and the United States.

The state reaches into family life in ways that are at once similar to, an intensification of, and a divergence from the effects of migration on relatedness. As with migration, these are families split by and transcending the U.S.-Mexico border,[19] but there is also a shift in the character of transnational families after deportation. In the aftermath of removal, families aim to reunite and hope to again create residences together, and the actions of migrants and their loved ones result in new and emergent forms of family. Yet when families are divided because of deportation, there are far fewer options for reunification—if any at all. Through removals, the state directly unravels kin networks across borders.

Through deportation, the state creates individual subjects in ways similar to other legal immigration processes, such as family reunification and naturalization as a U.S. citizen. Citizenship and immigration status are tied explicitly to individuals, underscoring how easily mixed-status families are created and reconfigured. Yet individuals are always embedded in broader familial ties and cannot—or should not—be disconnected from these family relationships.[20] Perhaps even more than immigration, deportation is experienced by a broad network of family members who profoundly feel its multiple effects. Through relatedness, deportation can become an assault on family life and one's place within kin relations. In the end, the state's removal of some family members is experienced within kin groups by all.

Any family member can essentially became "alien" by association,[21] through a process in which the unauthorized status of individuals is extended to others, symbolically and/or in concrete ways. Here, I build on Coutin's concept of alienation[22]—that is, the construction of an immigrant as "alien"—to explain how the state's making of "illegal aliens" can happen "precisely because of one's family relations."[23] The alienation of loved ones is possible because of undocumented migration but even more likely after deportation. Among family members of those deported, especially children and partners, the categories of "legality" and "illegality" are similarly linked to that of others. For example, this was clearly the case as Jaime's family ties were considered by the judge and ultimately deemed to be insufficient grounds for deferring removal. However, even when relations are determined to be "immediate" by the state, the likely outcome is family fragmented across borders.

In each of the families described in this chapter, kin continues to be a source of support from a distance, yet family members are indisputably divided. Jaime lives far from those he is closest to, even if the state challenged this fact. Emy's family is concentrated in Mexico, but her husband lives far away; their plans for future reunification remain uncertain. For Carlos, family is split down the middle: Carlos and Lucía and their youngest children are in Mexico, while three adult children and their partners and Carlos and Lucía's grandchildren are in the United States. In contrast, while Federico and Gaby have worked to reestablish a life in Mexico, their adult children travel back and forth when they are able to, albeit for limited periods. Federico realizes that he and Gaby may never again be in the United States. Still others, such as Antonia, must manage the challenges of an unanticipated reunion. Although the specifics of each family differ, deportation in all cases has tangible, disruptive results both geographically and temporally, including the jarring interruption of family ties, gender relations, spaces of home, and future aspirations.

PRECARITY

"Have you met your grandchild?," I asked, looking at a photograph of a smiling toddler standing in bright sunlight, her head tilted a bit to the side. I was talking with Alma, whose son, Tomás, had been deported after a routine traffic stop. Tomás had told me of the pain of being forced to leave his partner, Layci—who was pregnant with their first child—behind after the deportation. He wanted Layci, a U.S. citizen, to come with him to live in Mexico, but she said she could not bear to leave so many family members behind in order to follow another. This supposed "choice," Tomás explained, had not been an easy one. In the end, Layci stayed with her extended family—"left behind" in the United States—rather than leave with her new partner. She chose the assurance of a family network to help raise her daughter over the unknown configuration of unfamiliar in-law relations in an unfamiliar place. Meanwhile, Tomás found himself *solo,* all alone, in Mexico.

"Well, yes, of course I have met her!," continued Alma. "Through photographs . . . " She motioned to the image in my hand. "I have met Zoe through photographs. I know her through photographs." As Alma spoke, she used the verb *conocer,* which means "to meet" but also "to know." I was struck both by the hopefulness in her description of the relationship and by the precarity of the remote relations the photo symbolized: partners, father-daughter, grandmother-grandchild, all separated by borders but nonetheless understood as a network of tangible relations. Since the deportation, Tomás and Layci had communicated some, but the distance was stifling, and with no future plans to reunite the relationship had more or less dissolved. Taken from the possibility of a life with loved ones, Tomás passed time in rural Mexico while his one-time partner and young child went on without him in the United States. Tomás and Alma may never meet Zoe in person; they will likely continue to "see" and "meet" her in photos, or at least in the photos they already possess since such precarious ties are unlikely to endure. Theirs is another fragmented family—a family dispossessed of the possibility of reunification and unable to imagine, or actualize, a future path together.

The fragility of severed family ties—the direct result of the state's removal of a noncitizen of the nation regardless of any de facto membership—may be countered by a kind of fortitude, a new way of connecting across borders that results in new sorts of relationships. I repeatedly heard about these fragile yet enduring relationships created through phone calls and photographs, memories made or imagined through these sorts of abstract connections. One man, speaking of his nieces and nephews in the United States, assured me that he, too, had met family members born in *el norte*. "Well, we know them through photos," he explained. "But in person, no." Another couple told me of their four grandchildren living in Texas and Florida—all U.S. citizens. They, too, had met "only through photographs." It had been over fifteen years since their eldest son, Bruno, had gone to the United States, so they also relied on photos and phone calls to sustain their relationship with him. As his mother Marcia explained, Bruno had left at the age of fourteen, "still a child," and had "become a man" during his absence. This, she said, was painful in a way that can be difficult to articulate, but she was grateful for the photos, for she could see the man he had become.

Such fleeting connections—ties that despite material markers like photographs or telephone calls are ephemeral, tenuous, fragile—reflect the reality that families face in an age of deportation. As deportations increase, the possibility that people will have a number of these abstracted or remote relationships also increases and, with that multi-plication, already strained connections across time and space become increasingly more difficult to sustain. People continue to make these efforts, maintaining family ties via alternative ways of "knowing" someone that stand in for face-to-face or direct interactions. Those who can travel and those who are willing to risk travel across territorial spaces do so, or in cases when geographic migration is not possible or unlikely family is stitched together through photographs, videos, phone conversations, messages and remittances sent by others, gifts, or other objects that can move more easily across borders than migrants them-selves. These strategies aim to create presence out of absence.

To know one through photos rather than through the intimacies of daily exchange, then, shifts the character of and possibility for family ties. Fleeting connections reflect the fact that in these conditions family relations themselves are fragmented and underscore kinship more gen-erally as increasingly precarious. The result is a recasting of kin, where the default is absence accompanied by intermittent and fragmented con-tact that introduces the notion of intentional but precarious ties. As relationships are forged without face-to-face interactions—and with fewer possibilities for reunification than through migration—relation-ships are more likely to be temporary, disrupted, or unexpectedly sev-ered. The sense of geographic separation intensifies as hope of joining kin again in the future recedes. In this milieu of circulating photographs, memories, and palpable absence, social relations are constituted and reconstituted transnationally, but as photographs and memories fade, family ties can dissolve, at times indefinitely.

Precarious family ties underscore yet another inequality in the way "distance" is experienced by different transnational subjects. The migrants I describe have limited access to membership and immigration status that might enable frequent border crossings. In addition, in an age of increasingly globalized communication and technology, there are those with means and access to such technologies and those without. In another form of violence, as many throughout the world are able to connect to a global network of cell phones, the Internet, and other pos-sibilities, Alma, Tomás, and most of the migrants I know are not. Migrants in poor, rural communities are increasingly "left behind"— due to both lack of means and lack of infrastructure—from the poten-tial for connection through such technologies in the first place.

Deportation is nearly always framed by this intensified precarity of family life. As I learned again and again of relationships stitched together through images, brief and sporadic conversations, or an occasional video transported by a friend, I was reminded of a conversation I had had several months earlier with Blanca and Emy, shortly after Emy had been deported and returned to the community. Blanca told us about a woman in a neighboring town who had become pregnant while her husband was in the United States. "She has been telling everyone that she got pregnant by talking with her husband on the telephone!," Blanca recounted with dismay. "Can you imagine? People have told her that this isn't possible—that of course you need to be in the same place to get pregnant—but she insists that the baby is her husband's child." The women laughed at the absurdity of the suggestion, and Emy joked, "Well, my husband and I talk by phone almost every day, so I'll probably get pregnant with twins!"

Still, while the woman they described was surely aware of the impossibility of conception by telephone, there was a kind of logic to her account in the context of fragmented families that have so little to hold on to as they try to build and maintain relationships across the border. The pregnancy was, at least in part, the fallout of separation across time and space. The woman was expecting a baby who—had circumstances been different—most likely would have been fathered by her husband. For these and other families, immigration control and increased deportations directly translate as precarious ties.

During an especially somber conversation with one returnee, Violeta, she described the pain of halted movement between Mexico and the United States. She and her husband, Luis, both undocumented migrants, had spent nearly two years in *el norte,* leaving their young children in Mexico under the care of their grandparents. As Violeta explained, the distance had became too difficult to bear, and so she decided to return to Mexico while her husband stayed and continued to work and send remittances home. Violeta had been pregnant with their third child when she migrated south, and six months later she gave birth to a son, born in his father's absence. As months have passed with uncertainty about what will come next, Violeta, too, has introduced her husband to his son "through photographs." As they consider what to do, these images stand in for daily interactions. This is life in a form of limbo, the precarity of family, future, and place.

Here lives are limited by deportability and deportation actualized. The state's making of so many as displaceable and expendable—those who are cast outside the nation or trapped within it, separated from family and forced to depend on tenuous ties—creates a precariousness that cannot be denied. These are relations that are formed, eroded, re-created, and reimagined in a context in which state removal feels immi-nent, a threat actualized and experienced by families every day. For these families—and millions more—photographs and phone calls are all they have for now, perhaps all they might ever have of a particular rela-tionship with another. These configurations of family, like many aspects of deportation, are marked by a devastating unpredictability.

Above all, a relationship forged through images captures the precar-ity of relations undone by state actions. The forced returns and migra-tions of related individuals through and to unexpected or unpredictable locales trigger much suffering. Again, displacement and deportation create loss and a type of disappearance—of people from everyday lives, of someone there and then gone, of a relationship that will likely never be as it might have been. Much is lost, or more accurately, much is taken away. The state's removal of Tomás resulted in his departure from a life with two U.S. citizens he loved. This family connection is precarious, one that will perhaps be permanently absent or disappear completely—for Tomás and Layci but also for Alma and, of course, for little Zoe. She will grow up in her nation, never knowing, or at least not knowing as she might have, the father who once was. Everyone I spoke with described family as fragmented because of deportation, often irreparably so. For now, families will continue to be deunified, leaving us to wonder, when everything falls apart because of deportation, how or even will families be reunited once more?

CHAPTER 5

Disorientation

When I walk around here in Mexico, I feel very strange, almost dizzy.

—Marisol

Returning to a story once again, illuminating the lack of structure

For Jaime, who had lived in the United States since he was a toddler, deportation as a teenager was distressing and profoundly disorienting. Jaime was left at the border after his deportation, instructed by his father to head south to his parents' home community and the town where he himself was born. I first met Jaime when he was in elementary school. We kept in touch over the years and periodically reconnected at family events and celebrations in the United States, so it was a quite a surprise to meet up with him in Mexico following his deportation. When I saw him at the home of a family member shortly after he had "returned"—or more appropriately, had been forced to do so—he was quieter than usual, shocked by the sudden turn his life had taken. Each time we saw each other after that, he repeated the language of fragmentation: his life had come apart as a result of removal. He wasn't sure what to do next, how to imagine a future living outside of the only country he really knew.

After months in prison and federal immigration detention, Jaime found himself in rural Mexico, a place he could not remember and did not identify as home. Upon "repatriation" to his "hometown," Jaime had no memories of Mexico to draw on. Indeed, in one of our conversations in Mexico after the deportation, Jaime recounted his earliest memories as a child. He recalled standing in a mall in the United States, seeing an escalator for the first time. For Jaime, life and life's recollections began in *el norte*. Although he was reunited with his grandmothers and extended family members in Mexico, he was very far from those who had played a key role in his childhood and adolescence, his parents, siblings, girlfriend, peers—the family and friends who had provided support in his day-to-day life. Within a matter of months after being caught up in deportation proceedings, Jaime's kin and social networks were upended. Suddenly, it seemed to him, he was displaced in rural Mexico with no idea of what might come next.

At his deportation hearing, Jaime chose to speak in English and tried to explain to the judge that his life was rooted in the United States: "I told him that I didn't know anything about life in Mexico, that it would be very difficult for me to get along and to get used to it. But it didn't matter. It didn't help." The judge asked if Jaime could speak Spanish. Jaime replied, yes, he could, but he had never lived in Mexico, at least not since he could remember. The judge was frank with Jaime: "There is nothing I can do for you." Jaime's understanding of home, family, and belonging differed significantly from the way the legal framework—and this specific judge—imbued the same concepts with meaning. When Jaime was deported, the judge warned him not to return to the United States, urging him to consider Mexico as his place of incarceration.

And, indeed, for Jaime, Mexico was something of a prison. As he talked about the many ways his life changed after deportation, he described a sudden, jarring return to an unfamiliar place: the food seemed strange; he could not always follow conversations in Spanish; he found it difficult to relate to other youth in the rancho. He thought this was perplexing—after all, he grew up speaking Spanish and interacting with Mexicans living in the United States. Still, the shift was difficult to manage, and he longingly reminisced about home. He told me that he could identify with my young daughter who was attending kindergarten in Mexico, learning Spanish for the first time and trying to adjust to so many new experiences. He felt disconnected, like he did not belong.

Jaime described how when he first arrived in Mexico it was "really weird . . . 'cause, I wasn't used to it. I wasn't used to the electricity, or the water. I don't really like that part. You have to get more water, or sometimes the electricity goes out or I don't have signal on my phone. I wasn't used to any of that. It felt stressful at first." When he arrived in the rancho, he shuttled between the homes of his grandmothers, one frail and in a wheelchair and the other recovering from hip surgery. He talked about the embodiment of the change he was experiencing: "The work here—it's really tough. I've been working with my uncles, to get food for the cows. And the sun is hard, it burns you quick." He said that people view him as different. "But," he continued, "I've got to handle it here, I've got to take it." Jaime tried to be positive: "I have to get it through my head that I'm here, so . . . " His voice trailed off, and we sat in silence.

"Are there things you like about being in Mexico?," I asked after the pause. He again hesitated. "Ummm, I guess basically the freedom and that I don't have to worry about the immigration police," he said, laughing. "That is what makes you feel better. I'm in my state and nobody can take me out now!" He said that he was "really happy to meet the whole family." He described how he had been able to connect with cousins he never knew: "We all play soccer, we play volleyball, or we go out to the dances. We drink a little bit." Still, spending time with family in Mexico was bittersweet. "It is hard," he explained. He missed his family in the United States and the life he had left behind. In Mexico, Jaime seemed to be passing time, or actually "serving time" just as the judge had instructed him. Whenever I saw him, he seemed disoriented, claiming he felt uneasy. It was as though he was waiting either for a change in his status or a sense of belonging, neither of which seemed to arrive.

OUT OF PLACE

In the aftermath of deportation, whether their own or that of a family member, children and youth find themselves "out of place," dislocated from familiar geographies but also distanced from multiple forms of membership. Certainly, deportation has disorienting effects on people of all ages, but these effects can be especially intense in the case of young people in transnational and mixed-status families. Inflexibility and exclusion best describe the places—as both location and position—of the youngest migrants affected by deportation. In the wake of deportation, young people are dislocated from family, friends, and familiar settings, disoriented by the chaos of return. And the impact of deportation is not only experiential; it also has implications for citizenship and membership in all its manifestations—legal, social, cultural.

This discussion extends several of the arguments developed in earlier chapters but investigates children and youth as a site of intersection for the many effects of return outlined above. The transborder movement of children is a collateral outcome of the chaos and disruption that inevitably accompanies individual removals and other forms of forced movement. Age influences or even determines the locations and possibilities for membership among transnational migrants, often trumping citizenship, immigration status, or the circumstances that resulted in return. Regardless of formal membership—whether U.S. citizens or residents, undocumented migrants, DACAmented youth, or those who are transitioning across statuses—young people are alienated and marginalized, some serially, some simultaneously. The experiences of undocumented migrant youth who are de facto U.S. citizens and U.S. citizen children who have been de facto deported converge. The disorienting effects of removal are strikingly similar in both cases. In the aftermath of deportation, children, regardless of citizenship and reasons for return, are likely to experience common trajectories.

U.S. citizen children displaced through the deportation of others are, as discussed, made "alien" precisely through ties to migrant family members. This process, prominent in the lives of children with immigrant parents, is intensified in the context of deportation. For U.S. citizens, status can quickly shift after the deportation of a loved one, as they transition from being a member of the nation to being an exiled subject or de facto deportee. When U.S. citizen children and youth "return" to Mexico, they embody a further compromised form of citizenship, as their displacement from the United States may initiate their status as undocumented migrants in their parents' nation of origin.

In 2007, the Urban Institute and the National Council of La Raza estimated that two-thirds of children with deported parents are U.S. citizens.[1] In addition, a report by the Applied Research Center found that the number of families affected by deportation is increasing: between 1998 and 2007, 8 percent of deportees were parents of U.S. citizen children; in 2011, the figure rose to 22 percent.[2] The exact number of U.S. citizen children with a deported parent is difficult to estimate, but given that deportations are being carried out in record numbers, the figure is sure to be large.

Similarly, youth who are undocumented migrants in the United States can experience a form of exile and become "alien" when they move south, despite their indisputable, "documented" place in Mexico. The Pew Research Center estimates that 1.5 million undocumented migrants in the United States are children.[3] For those who migrated to the United States without authorization at a young age, "return" to Mexico—whether through their own deportation or that of a family member—presents yet another form of invisibility, even in a nation that is formally their own. Their welcome to unknown or previous communities can be not so welcoming, as they once again face the inhospitality extended to newcomers that they first experienced in the United States.

At a moment when youth throughout the world are increasingly taking part in global connections and exchanges, deportation can instead result in an experience of disconnection and severed ties across borders. Young people move through spaces of absence and presence in particular ways. Displacement, contingent citizenship, and the forced absence of millions of young people from the United States demonstrate how dislocation and disorientation come to be defining aspects of experience for children caught within the web of state removals. The movement of young people in a transnational space shapes their access to and exclusion from specific places but also national belonging and citizenship itself.

Exiled

For Emy's four U.S. citizen children, deportation was experienced as displacement. Having been deported after living in the United States for most of a fifteen-year period, Emy found it difficult to decide whether the children should stay in the United States with their father, Manuel—who, like Emy, is an undocumented migrant—or join Emy in Mexico. Recall that the children were with Manuel for about a month, but then the family made the necessary arrangements for a coyote to bring the children "back" to Mexico.

During one of my visits, I talked with two of Emy's children, Cora and Joaquín, about life in the rancho, and the prominent theme was that of "boredom." "I am soooo bored," Cora said, as she glanced up at me while painting her nails. Joaquín told me that he, too, was bored and preferred the United States but that at least he was now with his mother again. From the beginning, Cora was puzzled that I had chosen to spend a year living in Mexico, for she was there, she emphasized, against her will. She was happy to be living with her mother, but that was "the only good thing about it," she said. "I don't have anything to do!" She asked when I planned to return, and when I told her she quickly replied, "Take me! Please take me with you, *please!*" Repeatedly, Cora reminded me of the many ways she did not fit in: "At home, I was on the phone all the time, or texting. Now we don't even have phone reception. I hate school. I even got in a fight with another student. I am glad I can be with my mother, but I wish I were back in the U.S."

As Cora spoke, it was clear that she views Mexico as a liminal place, a place she inhabits while waiting to return to her home nation, the United States. She feels and is, like so many young people I spoke with, out of place. Born in California, Cora spent much of her childhood living in *el norte*. Although she lived briefly with her grandparents in Mexico when she was a preschooler, most of her schooling and upbringing has been in the United States. She prefers to speak English, she attended an urban middle school in the Midwest, and, before returning to Mexico, she spent much of her time with friends, going to the mall on weekends, and planning for school dances. After her mother's deportation, however, Cora's experience of adolescence was shaped by her sudden and unexpected move to Mexico. While isolation, distance, and boredom may be typical for many teenagers in the United States, much of Cora's uneasiness seemed the product of her displacement. Never did Cora describe Mexico as "home." Although she had spent periods of time there as a young child, she told me that home was the United States, her country of birth and the place where she belongs.

Scholars have often considered the notion of exile as reserved for those who are forced to leave their country because of state action (or inaction) or political beliefs. However, for young people, their own deportation or the deportation of a family member and a "return" to Mexico is often experienced as exile.[4] The uprootedness inherent in deportation is felt concretely by children and youth as they are displaced, excluded from the territory of the nation and no longer physically present or located there. Youth feel and are, in many ways, out of place, as they are "returned 'home' to a place where, in their memory [or in reality], they have never been."[5] Among young people the experience of exile is quick to cross lines of membership, as citizens of both the United States and Mexico share elements of this dislocation and place-based disorientation.

Although "we consciously read 'exile' as enforced displacement and dislocation,"[6] there is an elusiveness to exile and return. There are multiple "modalities of placement and displacement,"[7] and exile is not necessarily tied to a (or one) referent home or place.[8] As Hamid Naficy writes, these are "variegated exiles, big and small, external and internal, forced and voluntary."[9] Yet while "exile" as it has been defined and studied may not officially apply to displaced young people living in Mexico after deportation, exile understood as "political expulsion and banishment"[10] still resonates with them. The displacement of young deportees and the children of deportees is the result of particular state actions, and can guide us to reconsider the ways that current state practices and state control can indeed force individuals to leave their home nations.

U.S. citizen children affected by the deportation of others are, like the deported Salvadorans described by Coutin, "exiled by law."[11] The state converts U.S. citizens into exiles through restrictionist immigration laws and enforcement aimed at their family members. U.S. citizen children relocated to Mexico find themselves in a foreign place: most have never been to Mexico, English is likely to be their first or preferred language, educational institutions are unfamiliar to them, and they face challenges adjusting to a new place and new life. The children of deportees complicate the category "exile"; they fit the category in certain respects but also go beyond it, adding to our definition of exiled subjects in the twenty-first century.

Similarly, Mexican citizens whose upbringing took place mostly in the United States without authorization are also exiled. I was struck, for example, by the similarities between Jaime, an undocumented migrant who was deported, and Cora, a U.S. citizen who went to Mexico after her mother was deported. Both described being on the margins in Mexico, exiled citizens even if not formally so. They spoke of the disorienting elements of displacement, the confusion and cloudiness of being "placed" outside the borders of the United States, displaced from home, family, and nation. Although both Jaime and Cora have formal membership or access to it in Mexico (Jaime because of birthright citizenship and Cora through her parents, both of whom are Mexican citizens), it is not their de facto nation of belonging. Deportation is almost always displacement and exile, even when the destination is one of multiple homelands.

Transnational movement and displacement from their home nation can come to define life for children in mixed-status and migrant families, producing U.S. citizens who are de facto exiled but also exiled de facto U.S. citizens. For Jaime and the millions of other Mexican citizen children who left Mexico at a young age to begin a life in the United States, exile from Mexico was a first displacement; after a childhood in the United States, however, displacement was reversed. Displacement at a very young age, from south to north, can paradoxically produce further estrangement from home, such that exile for young people might become a way of life. A "return" to Mexico, even when it is one's nation of origin, can be experienced as exile rather than homecoming.

Similarly, U.S. citizens such as Emy's children may experience displacements in different directions even at a young age. I first met Emy's eldest children, Cora and Joaquín, when they were still preschoolers. Emy had brought them to Mexico to live with her mother, their grandmother, for two years while she worked in San Diego. At that time, Emy told me that her unauthorized status was too much of a risk for her children, and she feared what might happen to them if she were deported, an eerie foreshadowing of events that indeed came to pass. As U.S. immigration controls intensify—even more today than when Cora and Joaquín were living in the rancho years ago—the care of migrants' children is shifting to Mexico.[12] Fearing deportation, unauthorized migrants bring or send their children, especially very young children, to their home communities to stay with family members just as Emy did. And as deportations are on the rise, children increasingly experience displacement as they are formally or informally exiled from the United States.

Such displacement can even be experienced in the United States by children after the deportation of a parent. For example, as discussed earlier, at different stages after deportation, Federico's U.S. citizen children returned to the United States. But rather than a homecoming, they experienced a kind of exile in their own nation. Displaced not from their country of origin but instead from their family, they, too, experienced disorientation and dislocation. Federico and Gaby's daughters in Mexico also felt like exiles. The awkwardness of high school was compounded by the need to navigate an entirely new context of youth politics and interpersonal relations. Their youngest daughter described a school system that was especially unfamiliar, and each of the children in Mexico now had to study in a language they had previously only spoken.

The lives and experiences of transnational children challenge the definition and experience of exile as adhering only to people with membership status vis-à-vis economic or political participation. After deportation, young people are exiled in ways similar to political exiles, even if they are not forced to move across borders because of dissent against one's government or state impunity. Instead, state actions against children (and their parents) are perhaps less visible and transnational Mexicans' "resistance" to state power less explicit. Still, the collective experiences of children and youth, regardless of formal citizenship, demonstrate how the chaotic character of deportation's dis/placement is a form of exile not unlike that at other periods in the past. Indeed, the political circumstances within a particular nation-state at any given moment in history can force the movement of its citizens and residents to another place.

Each time I saw Cora she was withdrawn—as if she were an observer in her own home, a place she barely knew. Emy told me of the many challenges Cora was having in school, often speaking of it in front of her, as if she wasn't there: "*Oye,* the difficulties Cora has had! She was a good student in the United States, but now she struggles. And she fights with other students—can you imagine?" "Yeah, she even slapped a student," added her younger brother, Joaquín, in English. I looked over at Cora, sitting silently on her mother's bed. She shrugged her shoulders and rolled her eyes.

Another time when I talked with Cora and Joaquín, I brought disposable cameras for them. I suggested that they might help with my research, that they could take photos of places they liked or did not like in the rancho, places that meant something to them or perhaps images of people or objects that had come to be central since their move to Mexico. Initially, they seemed a bit perplexed. "I don't like anything here," said Cora without pausing. "Well," I replied, "you could take photos of things that are boring to you." She perked up: "That I will be able to do! I could take photos of school, for sure." "It sounds like school is difficult," I said. "Definitely," replied Cora. "I get so frustrated, so angry." Joaquín reminded me of the encounter he had mentioned earlier: "She hit someone, you know." This time, Cora did not look at me, and we did not speak about the details of the incident. I had a hard time aligning my knowledge of a quiet and bright girl with the description of this event, and indeed her family's repetition of the incident emphasized just how out of character it was for Cora. Yet her body language and her palpable frustration communicated that, for her, lashing out at a classmate who had said something or implied something about her might have been an expression of the convergence of standard adolescent frustrations and her particular situatedness as a reluctant migrant.

My interactions with Cora and Joaquín reminded me of a conversation I had had a decade earlier with the town's preschool teacher. At the time, Emy was working in the United States while Cora and Joaquín were in Mexico, living with their grandparents and an aunt. I recalled that the teacher expressed concern about what might happen with U.S. citizen children such as Cora and Joaquín. She said that they seemed to be struggling emotionally and socially—far from their parents, missing them and speaking of them often. Soon after that research trip to Mexico, the children traveled back to the United States with a family member who is also a U.S. citizen and were reunited with their parents. The next time they "returned" to Mexico was the trip that followed Emy's deportation.

After a few weeks, I came back to collect the cameras. Joaquín handed me his, smiling; he said he had taken many photos, most of sunsets but some of their corral, his mother and siblings, friends from school. But Cora decided not to take photos; she said she couldn't be bothered. She was in good spirits as we joked about it: she even found it boring to document the things that bored her. She told me that she was looking forward to her *quinceañera,* which was going to take place over the holidays. Her father planned to make the trip to Mexico, and there was even a chance that her best friend would travel south to attend. "But I don't know," she said, "we haven't talked in more than a month." The upcoming birthday celebration provided a distraction and promised, or at least hinted at, a reconnection with her previous life. Yet the uncertainty of her good friend's visit reaffirmed that Cora was living in exile— far from her nation and her primary peer social network, in an unfamiliar place with no immediate plans for return.

Undocumented Deportation

As teenager Marisol recounted her return south, she described the shock of arriving in rural Mexico: "I looked around, and thought, 'Well, this is very different from Dallas!' It was a tiny town surrounded by farms— it was cute but *very* different." After growing up in urban Texas from the time she was a toddler, Marisol—like Jaime, Cora and Joaquín, and Federico's children—found rural Mexico disorienting. "When I told my parents I was surprised to see where I would be living, they said, 'Well, actually, this isn't it . . . we still need to travel to the rancho.' Then, after a long time driving down dirt roads, we arrived . . . I saw all the dust, the farm animals, and I couldn't believe it. I didn't like it. I felt so odd. It seemed very ugly to me. I told my parents, 'No, I want to go back!' This was where I was going to live, but it didn't seem real. I just couldn't believe how everything had changed."

Marisol's father, Carlos, was deported after several attempted crossings into the United States following the death of his father. Marisol's mother and younger siblings went to Mexico shortly after the deportation, but Marisol stayed on, for a while at least. Her parents wanted her to graduate from high school, and since Marisol had migrated to the United States at such a young age, she had no memories of Mexico and wanted to stay with her older siblings and friends. Marisol is a Mexican citizen, and an unauthorized migrant in the United States, but her understandings of Mexico were crafted and fostered by her parents through stories and their memories of their small, rural community rather than her own experience. For Marisol, Mexico was a place only imagined, a place that seemed far from her de facto home nation, the United States.

After Carlos's deportation, Marisol first spent two years living with her sister and family in Texas, until her parents decided it was time for Marisol, too, to "return" to Mexico. Having their daughter, now a young woman, living in the United States without their close supervision was a source of stress to Marisol's parents, so they brought her "home." Marisol was happy in Texas, and at first resisted her parents' requests that she join them. "But in the end," she told me, "they convinced me to come to Mexico." As Emy and Manuel did with their children, Carlos and Lucía made plans for Marisol to cross the border from north to south with a coyote of sorts: in their case, they arranged for a family friend, a U.S. permanent resident, to bring Marisol to their community. Because the town is accessible only by unpaved roads, the family met Marisol in a neighboring town just off the highway, this first "out-of-the-way place"[13] where Marisol described feeling "odd" and disoriented.

Like Cora and Joaquín, Marisol's life was disrupted by her forced—or at least not voluntary—relocation to Mexico. She, too, told me in English that she is "bored" living in Mexico, "*really* bored." I asked what she did during her first weeks "back" in her hometown. "Nothing much," she replied. "I rode around on scooters with another teenager who had spent time in the United States. At first, I really didn't want to be here." From Marisol's perspective, the United States is home. She told me that she spent her first months in Mexico distraught and wanting to go back to Texas. Marisol described how challenging it was to connect with people in the rancho; she saw them as "very different" and lamented that "nothing is the same here." She talked about the many opportunities in the United States that she did not have in Mexico, "opportunities to get ahead." But, she explained, "in the U.S. you need papers. Everything depends on the papers." The United States, then, is a home that Marisol acknowledges she has limited access to.

Marisol was subject to what I consider an *undocumented deportation*. As an undocumented migrant who followed a deported parent to Mexico, she does not show up in any formal accretion of statistics. This experience stems from the fact that although Marisol is an undocumented migrant, she is in many ways a de facto U.S. citizen. Kanstroom identifies the "*de facto* deportations" of U.S. citizens that often follow the formal deportation of family members.[14] For U.S. citizen children, such as Cora and her siblings, this concept of de facto deportation resonates. Their "return" was a kind of deportation, albeit one through informal channels.

Extending Kanstroom's argument about the de facto deportations of U.S. citizens, such informal or undocumented deportation can also forcibly relocate those who are not U.S. citizens. As I have argued, experience converges despite different citizenships or immigration statuses, so children of those who are deported, U.S. citizens and undocumented migrants alike, can find themselves similarly "deported," even if their removals are not recognized or directly carried out by the state. Among young people, undocumented deportation shares much with state-enacted deportation. For example, when Cora and Marisol were informally deported, they went through many of the same experiences that Jaime did when he was formally removed by the U.S. government. The lines that divide state removals from undocumented deportations repeatedly blur.

Undocumented deportations and undocumented migrations also have several common aspects. Both happen under the radar, outside the formal channels of the state. Both forms of movement may require guides or coyotes to facilitate border crossings, especially among those understood as vulnerable, such as the very young and the elderly. Just as undocumented migrations can result in lives undeniably (though unofficially) rooted in the United States, undocumented deportations can translate into concrete removals from the state's territory. And, significantly, although undocumented movement in both directions is outside of state systems, unauthorized migrations north and undocumented deportations south similarly serve the U.S. state and especially its economy, such that they might be better understood as what Luis Plascencia calls "informally authorized" forms of movement.[15]

Undocumented deportations, especially of U.S. citizens, call into question the foundation of citizenship itself. This conundrum reveals that full membership in the nation is possible for some citizens, but not for all. Are there, as Homi K. Bhabha asks, "those who must be displaced—at home and abroad—to constitute the 'good' people, the right 'stock,' the true blood, the civilized?"[16] And how are children and youth redefined and recategorized so as to be among those expelled from the nation? Discourse about the perceived growing "Latino threat"[17] and legislation aimed at excluding unauthorized migrants from opportunities, education, and forms of social support erode citizenship and result in the exile and undocumented deportation of young people.

Current debate about birthright citizenship also illustrates this point. Politicians who suggest rescinding birthright citizenship and the refusal of some counties to even issue birth certificates to the children of undocumented migrants underscores how these children do not, in practice, have access to full membership in the nation; their authenticity as members of the nation is questioned. The citizenship of children born in the United States to undocumented migrant parents may be informally revoked through the construction of "alien citizenship,"[18] or, as proposed in current political debate, could potentially be formally withdrawn by redefining national membership. The growing number of children who are taken from their homes and placed in foster care when their parents are deported[19] further reveals citizenship's contingency. Deportees may be deemed unfit parents because of undocumented migration and may lose custody of their children. Children may be temporarily separated or even permanently severed from their parents. This model implies that U.S. citizenship of young people can be reconstituted only if the state cuts the ties of parent and child and places the child in a family of U.S. citizens.

Undocumented deportations, then, reveal the instability of national membership, for all migrants regardless of citizenship but especially for young people whose upbringing has straddled two countries. For youth who are deported, but also for young people related to deportees, membership is precarious and tenuous. Here, belonging can be disorienting, leading to a form of doubly dislocated citizenship. In previous work, I have described the ways that, through relatedness, migrant children and the children of migrants may have a form of *contingent citizenship,* or "national membership that is partial, conditional, or relational."[20] Similarly, through deportation, the national membership of young people is directly linked to the immigration status of others, especially parents. If detention and deportation are processes through which the state is squarely situated in intimate relations of family, undocumented deportations extend the state's presence even further into everyday lives.

For Marisol, for example, state controls are ever-present, even thousands of miles from the United States. The state's categorization of Marisol and her parents and siblings as "alien"—and later, her father's movement through categories of "deportable" to "deportee"—overtly influenced their daily lives while living in Texas. But U.S. state categories continue to shape Marisol's experiences of belonging and exclusion in Mexico. The construction of a member of the nation as "alien"— whether as undocumented migrant or undocumented deportee—is attached not only to one's own status but also to the statuses of one's family members.

The resulting precarity is a form of what the sociologists Cecilia Menjívar and Leisy J. Abrego term "legal violence,"[21] as state categorization—meant to delineate status along clear lines—is anything but clearcut. The concepts "vulnerable stability"[22] and "liminal legality"[23] capture the fluidity and contradictions of state-ascribed and ostensibly fixed legal categories. Yet while Menjívar and Abrego focus primarily on the shifting and nebulous position of those with Temporary Protected Status or other forms of temporary relief from deportation,[24] liminal legality can also extend to U.S. citizens. Scholars have shown differences among the advantages and disadvantages of children in mixed-status families based on immigration status.[25] Curiously, deportation also results in a kind of unjust equalizing, through which the status of all family members may be reduced to that of noncitizen or deportee, with an accompanying denial of the full rights of U.S. citizenship.

These shifting categories of membership and immigration status lead to "lives in limbo."[26] Status applies to and has an impact on the youngest migrants in particular ways; "return" for children is most often de facto or undocumented deportation. This expansive production of "illegality" and the way it extends and travels along family ties directly shape the trajectory of young people—through migration, certainly, but perhaps even more through deportation. For example, Marisol, already an undocumented migrant, became an undocumented deportee following the deportation of her father. The alienation caused by her undocumented migration was extended or compounded due to state removal, since Marisol's primary identification was attached to living in the United States. The restricted citizenship of young people is, of course, most pronounced among undocumented youth, but even U.S. citizen children such as Cora and Joaquín find themselves moving, not moving, or being forced to move within this frame of inflexibility. In the current milieu, young people of diverse citizenships and statuses may embody a space of alterity, within the nation and, increasingly, outside it.

As I spoke with Marisol's mother, Lucía, her three-year-old son, Nico—Marisol's younger brother—played quietly nearby. Even though Lucía repeatedly described the many challenges the family had faced since coming back to Mexico, she remained hopeful that Nico, a U.S. citizen and the only sibling in the family with this status, would one day return to the United States. Yet Nico's experience thus far was in keeping with that of his family members, including Marisol, who did not have authorization to live in the United States. Nico has been expelled—albeit informally so—from the United States, forced to live outside his nation of origin after his de facto deportation. He is, significantly, a subject whose membership in both nations is compromised: like Marisol was, he is being raised outside of the nation of his birth and citizenship.

Should Nico return to the United States at some point in the future, it will likely seem as alien to him as Mexico does to Marisol.

Seeing little Nico run around his family's courtyard with a small truck, mimicking the sound of a revving engine, it was difficult to perceive him as an exile or undocumented deportee. Of course, the long-term trajectory of Nico and other U.S. citizens is distinct: they can cross the border and reside in the United States without the same dangers and risks that undocumented migrant children face. Still, although U.S. citizenship can facilitate safer passage across the border and entry into the country, what kind of return might it be? In Nico's case, after living most of his childhood in Mexico, will movement north be a return, a homecoming, a kind of new migration? After formal or undocumented deportation, children are displaced and exiled: in the United States one day, gone the next. Similarly, citizenship is compromised for all children who "return." Regardless of formal membership, categories of citizen or noncitizen can be rendered secondary, as the experience of belonging is complicated by years spent living in different countries and as relatedness to those deported or at risk of being deported erodes membership.

DECOSMOPOLITANIZATION

A large group gathered in a courtyard filled with flowers to celebrate a recent baptism, eating *gorditas* (cornmeal cakes) and *elote* (grilled corn on the cob) and catching up. Simón, a migrant I first met in the United States, greeted me, grinning and shaking my hand firmly. The event was festive and filled with activity as women bustled around preparing boxes of food that would be transported north the following day, care packages for those in the United States who had not been to Mexico for several years and who could not easily travel there because of their undocumented migrant status. Many of those in attendance lived in the United States and, as U.S. citizens and U.S. permanent residents, had papers that facilitated frequent border crossings, but many more, undocumented migrants, had not been able to make the trip to Mexico.

Family members had come together for this important celebration, a baptism ceremony for three children in an extended family: Simón's four-year-old son, Lorenzo, a U.S. citizen; Diego, Simón's seven-year-old nephew, also a U.S. citizen, with undocumented migrant parents in the United States; and a niece, Lila, a Mexican citizen who had just turned one year old. Simón, a naturalized U.S. citizen, had traveled to

Mexico with his wife, children, and nephew. Family members who could be in attendance were, but those who were most vulnerable vis-à-vis the U.S. state were unable to travel to Mexico for this rite of passage, having chosen not to take the risk. This was an unusual baptism in some respects, though perhaps given the increase in deportations and the high stakes of deportability, such transnational baptisms are likely to become more and more common.

The extended family was celebrating the three children, each in different circumstances with diverse combinations of citizenship and U.S. immigration status. Lorenzo is a U.S. citizen, as are all of his immediate family members. Diego, too, is a U.S. citizen, although his parents are not; they were unable to travel to the gathering given the risk of deportation should they attempt reentry, so Diego had traveled with his uncle Simón and cousins. And in Lila's family, no one has state authorization to migrate to the United States; in fact, her father was "removed" at the U.S.-Mexico border while trying to migrate north. He had tried to migrate when he was a young man but was unable to successfully cross and was "returned" by U.S. Border Patrol agents after several attempts. Discouraged by the removal, he had headed south to his town, remaining there and eventually marrying and starting a family.

One of the guests of honor, Diego, was visiting Mexico for the first time. He had never met his grandparents or other family members in his mother's hometown, and his parents had made arrangements for Simón to bring him to meet them and, his grandmother explained, to "get to know life in Mexico." Everything was new to Diego, and he looked stunned when I met him. I approached him and spoke in English. He nodded but said very little. After a minute, he walked off and stood by himself at the edge of the courtyard. "I am a little worried about him," said his grandmother Elena, watching him on the margins of the festivities. "He is supposed to stay with us for the next month and travel back to the United States with a cousin after his visit." Simón joined the conversation: "Diego spent much of his childhood in daycare centers with only English speakers, so while he understands Spanish from his parents, he does not speak it well."

The next week, I again went to talk with Diego and his grandparents. Now, all was quiet in the courtyard, and everyone except Diego had gone back to the United States. Elena served soft drinks and invited me to sit down, but Diego did not join us. As he had at the party, Diego stood at the gate leading into the family's property, kicking dirt and staring at his shoes. "I'm not sure what to do," said Elena. "I suppose we are getting to know him," she smiled. "But he is very quiet, so we aren't talking much!" The baptism of the three cousins with different statuses and likely radically different trajectories—and the position of Diego, out of place in his parents' hometown and unable to communicate easily with his family in Mexico—illustrates the ways that deportation and deportability affect children and youth, the complexities of citizenship in transnational and mixed-status families, and the particular marginalization that young people often experience. These children are betwixt and between two nations—members of one or two nations but also on the margins of both countries despite formal citizenship or status.

The young people I have discussed are familiar with the notion of (not) belonging in two places. Although home can be situated in multiple nations, they often are perceived as, or even understand themselves to be, "alien" in two countries. This is a form of abjectivity rooted in marginalization,[27] as children and youth find themselves located on the edges of global citizenship. In previous work I have written about *alien citizens* and *citizen aliens* produced by immigration,[28] but an age of deportation is intensifying this experience and broadening the categories. Each of the children baptized in the transnational ceremony I described above have compromised relationships—albeit to varying degrees—to two nations and their place in the world. While the cousins' statuses are transnational, a cosmopolitanism characterized by agency, fluidity, and opportunity cannot be said to attach to all of them equally. Because of his U.S. citizenship and that of his parents, Lorenzo has relative flexibility to move between the two countries and create home in both places, notwithstanding the increasing violence that limits migration for everyone. For Lila, the ability to cross the U.S.-Mexico boundary is extremely limited, despite the fact that much of her extended family live in the United States; even without formal authorization, however, she and/or those she is related to may migrate at some point in the future. Diego's status is liminal despite his U.S. citizenship. The vulnerable position of his parents, both of them undocumented migrants living in *el norte,* means that where he is likely to be placed (and potentially displaced) is uncertain. And regardless of where Diego resides, his membership in any one nation is tenuous and contingent.

Of course, these young people are in certain ways cosmopolitans, global citizens who have access to more than one culture or geography. Yet while youth throughout the world are increasingly taking part in global connections—including "imagined cosmopolitanism"[29]—for young transnational Mexicans, as well as others around the globe who share similarly tangled migration histories, *decosmopolitanization* is perhaps a more fitting description. Theirs is the contradictory experience of simultaneous cosmopolitanism and forced transnational movement. While the anthropologist Julia Meredith Hess illustrates how Tibetans can be "'at home' . . . in their diasporic identities,"[30] transnational Mexican children and youth affected by deportation are repeatedly alienated from transnational lives and identities, both by forcible removal that targets them and through the displacement of others. Cosmopolitan experience may promise to be an antidote to the divide "between 'us' and 'them,'"[31] but it remains an abstract and ever deferred promise as deportations challenge, weaken, and distance young people from this status.

In the cases documented here and countless cases like them, young people have limited access to cosmopolitanism and their place as "citizen[s] of the world."[32] Their feelings of being out of place reflect a much broader process of exclusion and are "the embodiment of a forced transnationality."[33] As young people are forced to move from urban centers in the United States to rural areas in Mexico, they experience an exile by means of which their claims to cosmopolitanism—already limited—are nearly stripped from them completely. Their difference, expressed by others and by young people themselves, and the "boredom" they describe seem to signal a shifting global order, one in which disorder and dislocation come to define place and position. Here, young people are constructed as "matter out of place."[34] As youth spoke of the "boredom" connected to returning and being returned, I came to interpret this trope to be about the condition of displacement and its attendant denial of membership. "Boredom" is often a narrative that for young people signals estrangement and the alienation that follows deportation.

Thus the context wherein young people move transnationally might be best understood as decosmopolitanization within a supposedly cosmopolitan milieu. Although transnational youth are often cosmopolitans through experience, they can be—especially because of deportation—shut out from the flexibility and benefits of such ostensibly global citizenship. Jaime, deported to Mexico by the U.S. government, Cora, a U.S. citizen and migrant to Mexico, and Marisol, a Mexican citizen and undocumented deportee, are each tied to two nations, yet curiously constructed as "alien" in both places. This is an experience described by children and youth but also by others around them. For example, several women in town told me that they perceive Marisol as "different" from their own daughters. They described being uncomfortable because Marisol is "always in the street" and because she appeared to be "pretentious." Marisol, however, told me that people in town initially seemed "envious" of her and that people did not seem to respect her. She has since made friends with other teenagers there, but she felt especially awkward in those first months. Similarly, Cora and Jaime were on the margins of the community after their return: Cora spoke of conflicts at school with other students, and Jaime said he had difficulties connecting with other youth.

What is read by others as Marisol's "pretension" is in part her position as a cosmopolitan, albeit in a compromised form. Her status, like the other young people I describe, does not neatly fit within "universalist claims to world citizenship"[35] but rather is a life undeniably rooted in transnational experience.[36] Far from the multiple-passport holders that Aihwa Ong portrays,[37] Marisol and her peers are cosmopolitans in a much more restricted and perhaps less glamorous sense. This is the terrain of "discrepant cosmopolitanisms"[38] that are "not only the practices of metropolitan elites but also the province and the project of particular, local, and less privileged sectors."[39] Cosmopolitanisms "can be done in diverse ways,"[40] and can potentially be undone as well.

Thus not everyone has the same access to cosmopolitanism, even as actual lives would seem to exemplify its spirit or promise. This disconnect is especially evident in the experience of youth, who at once embody the optimism of a cosmopolitan world and the ways that this hope for another path is repeatedly compromised. While transnational youth are often cosmopolitans by experience, they are—especially because of deportation—also precisely those who are shut out from the flexibility of such citizenship.[41] As Karen Kelsky outlines, "some citizens are more flexible than others,"[42] revealing how national sovereignty leads to "the terrible asymmetries of the idea of modernity itself."[43] The daily lives of children and youth who are affected by deportation repeatedly make this point.

When I asked Jaime which nation—Mexico or the United States—he was "from," he didn't hesitate: "I feel like I am North American, from the U.S., because of the way I lived over there, and the way I live here." In a sense, Jaime is a citizen, or perhaps more aptly, denizen, of the world, a cosmopolitan who has lived a life connected to multiple places and characterized by cross-border movement. Still, he is a citizen of no one place, as his claims to full membership in Mexico or the United States are limited. I reminded him of a comment he had made a few weeks earlier. "You said that you didn't remember the rancho before coming back." "Yeah," Jaime sighed. "I still don't."

In one of our many conversations about her children, Emy described the challenges of enrolling them in school in Mexico. She had assumed it would be a straightforward process, that the children would start school as soon as they arrived and without much effort. But the Mexican educational system proved to be more bureaucratic than she had anticipated, and the required paperwork, such as birth certificates and school transcripts, were very difficult to obtain, especially for Emy living as a deportee outside of the United States. Emy explained that she was working on acquiring the necessary documents and that fortunately—because they lived in a small community and knew the teachers well—her children were able to attend school while Emy straightened this out. But according to school administrators, the children could not be officially enrolled and would not receive credit for their coursework until their files were complete.[44]

In addition to being evidence of the unexpected quotidian hardships for returning migrants, Emy's difficulty with school enrollment underscores how U.S. citizen children living outside the nation may become undocumented migrants in Mexico, not unlike their family members living in the United States without formal membership. Currently the world's "horizon is marked, all at once, by the spirit of arrival and the spectre of departure."[45] This "spectre of departure" reveals the instability of the supposedly fixed category of legal citizenship. The experiences of young people exiled to Mexico raise questions about the place of transnational subjects in an age of deportation, demonstrating the contingency of citizenship itself.

ABSENCE

For Tomás, life has been defined by sudden shifts in absence and presence. At the age of thirteen, he disappeared from one life in Mexico, appeared in the United States and created a life there, only to be deported and sent back to Mexico before his eighteenth birthday, absent from a life lived once again. Tomás was literally taken from one place and plopped down in another, finding himself out of place twice over. First, he vanished from an adolescence in Mexico, taken—or more aptly, trafficked—to the United States by a businessman from a neighboring town who owns a chain of restaurants. Tomás told me that he and a friend "were contracted to work in the United States," though this took place outside of formal state authorization. Tomás described the thrill, but also the anxiety, of traveling to the border and then being flown in a small jet—the pilot was a *"gabacho"* (white U.S. citizen) who only spoke English—to their new place of employment. For the first month and a half, their entire salary went to pay for the passage that had been arranged by the restaurant's owner. Living above the restaurant in an apartment with eight other young men, Tomás spent his first years in the United States with a very limited footprint or presence there, rarely leaving the building where he worked and slept.

After several years in California, Tomas's brother convinced him to move to Texas for better work opportunities and so that the siblings could be reunited. But Tomás found Texas "awful" when he compared it to California, which he thought was far preferable for undocumented migrants. Within six months of moving to Texas, Tomás was to become absent once more, removed from the United States by federal agents. The removal happened quickly. One weekday before sunrise he was headed to work, a well-paying job operating a forklift at a large construction site, when the police stopped him. Tomás had been driving to and from work without a license because as an undocumented migrant he could not get one. The police cited him and told him he was required to appear in court in order to pay the fine.

Because he had Christmas Eve off, Tomás—accompanied by two friends he planned to spend the holiday with—went to court to comply with the citation. Immediately, all three men were detained, first by the police and then by immigration officials. "I asked why I was being held, and they told me, 'This is Immigration.' They said it could be easy for me—that I could sign something if I wanted to leave voluntarily. They told me that if I wanted to have a hearing, I would be charged thousands of dollars per week for my stay in detention. So I said, 'Well, then I want to go voluntarily,' and so I signed." Daunted by this misinformation and the threat of "fees," Tomás waived his right to a hearing and was removed. "I spent Christmas and New Year's Day in detention," he told me. Tomás was only seventeen years old at the time and should have gone through a different process specifically for minors, which might have meant a different outcome, but no one ever asked his age.

"They put us on a bus and took us to the border. You know how they are there," Tomás said. Like other migrants who have been detained, he described chaos: "A lot of us lost our things. People grabbed the wrong bags. Luggage was being moved around." It was on the bus, amid this commotion and confusion, that Tomás lost the few possessions he still had by then: the documents outlining his removal and a ring of keys. He sighed, "But, well, I guess that doesn't matter now." I asked if he thought his experience of return was similar to Jaime's and Marisol's. Tomás felt it was perhaps even more difficult for them, "because they went when they were very young. They grew up there [the United States]. I think it is hard to come here [Mexico] suddenly." Still, while Tomás distinguished between his return and that of Jaime and Marisol, it seemed a difference of degree rather than kind. Tomás, too, described jarring shifts as he went absent at different times: first "suddenly," from a life in Mexico, and then again, from the United States, from the life he had built, albeit tenuously. In a matter of hours he was taken from his partner and soon-to-arrive daughter with no idea if he would ever return.

For children and youth, country of residence and citizenship can be disrupted, suspended, or upended because of deportation, as location quickly shifts from lives once known. The young people I have described often find themselves disoriented in terms of both place and belonging, even at times despite formal status vis-à-vis the state. Here, U.S. citizens, including Federico's children, Emy's children, Diego, and little Nico, *and* undocumented migrants such as Jaime and Tomás—themselves deported—and Marisol—who experienced an undocumented and unrecorded deportation—can be similarly exiled and displaced, marginalized from full membership in any one nation.

All of these young people—through their own deportation or the deportability or deportation of others to whom they are related—had lives suddenly defined by, and as a type of, absence. Displaced from their homes and from the nation where they definitively place or assign themselves, they entered a kind of void precipitated by "deportation not as a *return* but as a *departure*."[46] They are "situated in multiple places and nowhere at the same time."[47] That is, they are gone from one local community and present in a new place but always caught in an "in-between" space[48] that defines their transnational lives.

Like the refugees that Liisa Malkki describes, youth affected by deportation "occupy a problematic, liminal position in the national order of things."[49] Such liminal spaces are familiar to Cora, Marisol, Jaime, Tomás, and other young people: each had lives firmly rooted in the United States, but after deportation, lives continued without them. They went "missing" in a sense,[50] leaving behind what Sunaina Marr Maira calls the "presence of someone or something not completely there."[51] This absence is never fully remedied by presence elsewhere; "home" can rarely be actualized in the sense that the proximity of family, formal national membership, and geographic placements are not likely to ever again converge after deportation. Some (or all) elements will always be out of place.

Young people affected by deportation therefore cannot be easily placed in several senses. They are displaced in a literal sense, living somewhere they do not view as home. They are similarly out of place and disoriented in terms of experience, where all seems foreign, strange, or different. And, finally—and significantly—they are displaced in terms of positionality or "social locations,"[52] cosmopolitans but not entirely. This raises the question, where do these children "belong"? They may be at home in both places or inhabit an "interstitial" or "Third Space,"[53] but notably, they are not fully recognized members of any one country. Removal, and its many returns, reveals the instability of the supposedly fixed category of legal membership or even an ostensibly permanent process such as deportation.

This context of absence and disorientation is a setting in which young people can be displaced unexpectedly and abruptly. For now, Nico continues to live in his parents' hometown, although the chance for return to the United States remains. For his sister, Marisol, a future return is less likely because she does not have U.S. citizenship, but it is still a possibility. Tomás has decided to stay in Mexico, but he has not ruled out that he might migrate north again. Joaquín told me he is fine living in the rancho for the time being, but his sister Cora still laments her absence from the United States. Jaime continues to hold on to life in *el norte* through occasional phone calls with his girlfriend and family members and still does not feel at home in the nation he is formally from.

What does the future hold for displaceable, displaced, and deported young people? What will become of this generation of U.S. citizen children growing up in Mexico? How will lives unfold for the undocumented migrant children living in Mexico with deported parents? And, finally, when migrants themselves are deported at a young age, will migrations continue despite this status of deportee, a category that signals new forms of liminality? The sudden shifts of absence and presence are disorienting as children and youth find themselves dislocated in multiple senses. Even if they return "home" or migrate again at some point in the future, theirs are lives altered by deportation. As deportations increase, the "erasures of presence"[54] for young people are many. Increasingly, for the growing numbers of children and youth who cross borders in the aftermath of deportation, their migrations are outside the law and their destinations far from their nation. Furthermore, the experiences of young people affected by deportation raise questions about national membership more generally and about its elusiveness for all transnational subjects, even at times regardless of age, status, or migration trajectory.

. . .

On different occasions, Marisol described the experience of disorientation, a feeling of being on the perimeter of the community in both the United States and Mexico. Like Cora, she seemed to be on the outside looking in. In the United States, she told me, she had definitely felt left out at times, primarily because she did not have "the papers that are so important there." Still, her closest friends when she was growing up in Texas, the kids she felt most connected to and with whom she identified, were the U.S. citizen children of immigrants. In many ways, Marisol was positioned as her friends were and still are. Marisol's experience was that of a child of immigrants and not as an immigrant herself; she is much more like a member of the "second generation,"[55] but without papers, experienced as a practical problem with lasting effects, she is not formally part of it.

I asked how it felt to leave the United States, how it was during her first days back in Mexico. "Very strange," she replied. "Wherever I went, I felt like I was watching everything around me. But with time, little by little—*little by little*—I hope I will get used to it here. In Mexico, I feel 'leftover'—is that how you say it?" Although most of our conversation had been in Spanish, she interjected the word *leftover* in English. "Overlooked?," I asked. "Yes, maybe that," said Marisol, again speaking in Spanish. "I feel cast aside or left behind, like no one pays attention to me. It is like no one sees me."

Another time, when Marisol came to visit my family in Zacatecas, she again talked about estrangement as we walked through the streets of the city. She had come to research schools where she might study hairstyling. She had started in a program in Texas but had to drop out rather suddenly when she returned to Mexico. As we went from school to school, gathering information about the cost and duration of each program, Marisol said that she felt out of place and quite "dizzy." She asked if we could sit down for a moment. Fittingly, she used the word for motion sickness, *mareada,* to describe her movement to and through unfamiliar places. She said she felt odd in Zacatecas—it was a city with a lot people, yet no one knew her. "But in the rancho I feel odd, too. There, I feel strange because there are so *few* people." She laughed at the seeming contradiction, but it was an accurate description of her new place in the world. Marisol was "invisible" in both settings, absent from each place even as she was present in them. She felt, and in fact was, very far from home.

CHAPTER 6

Reinventions

Who knows what the future will bring?

—Lucía

Near the end of my extended fieldwork in Mexico, I visited with Rodrigo and Teresa. They were among the first migrants I interviewed about the effects of deportation, and their "removal" was especially perplexing because they had been sent back while attempting to enter the United States with a valid tourist visa. They were returned while following the law and, as discussed, experienced a kind of betrayal by the legal process. Although they have many family members in the United States, they had not attempted reentry. For the time being, they said, they planned to remain in Mexico.

It was midsummer, and families throughout the region were in a particularly busy period of the agricultural cycle. Community members were grateful for heavy rain and were working around the clock to ensure that the variety of pinto beans grown throughout the region—called *flor de mayo*—was planted during the small window of time that would facilitate a bountiful harvest in September. Although it was after 10:00 p.m. and already dark, they suggested we take a trip to the milpas on the perimeter of the community to check on the family's plot of land. Rodrigo and Teresa's sons were planning to work late into the night, guided by a large floodlight. The group quickly grew: in addition to me and my family, there were several of Rodrigo and Teresa's children, grandchildren, and nieces and nephews, including some visitors from California and New Mexico.

We piled into two pickup trucks and started down a dirt road in the direction of the family's farm. The collective mood was cheerful, almost celebratory, as we drove through the outskirts of town until there were no structures in sight. The night was warm and the sky clear, with stars in every direction. As adults chatted and children giggled, I talked with Teresa about life in Mexico since the deportation. She was hopeful that this year's harvest would be successful and that there would be enough to provide for their needs. They were also fortunate to have ongoing ties to the north, including family members who could send remittances if resources were to become tight. We rocked back and forth along the bumpy road as we made our way to the farmland that circled the small town.

At one point, the front tire of the pickup I was riding in hit a large boulder, throwing several passengers from one side of the truck bed to the other. Everyone laughed as they again found a spot for the ride. I looked in the milpas and saw that they were filled with rocks of various sizes, some quite large. "You can farm in such rocky soil?," I asked. Teresa looked at me and smiled, "Well, of course, if you can move the rocks, you move them. But if you can't, you leave them where they are and plant around them." It was a simple point, but I was struck by how it spoke to the lives of those affected by return. Removal places rocks in life's way. As those who have been deported and their loved ones experience firsthand, sometimes you can move the rocks and reconfigure multiple elements of daily life: family members re/locate across nations, livelihoods from the past such as farming can again become central, and where and how to care for loved ones draws on familiar strategies. In other circumstances, the options are very limited or the barriers insurmountable, so you leave behind aspects of a life that once was and create a place in the world for yourself that is entirely new. Regardless, forced return forces a recasting of oneself. The rocks do not disappear; they are moved aside, if possible, but ever a permanent part of the landscape.

· · ·

This book shows the chaos that frames deportation and its aftermath. As the lives of migrants make clear, these are uncertain returns: along temporal scales, through the un/predictability of locations of residence, with the construction of some subjects as recognized members of the nation and others as not. When individuals are directly expelled from the country and their loved ones are forced to leave with them, presence is unmade, and so are gendered kin relations, people's understandings of their place in the world, and even citizenship itself. Migrants face new insecurities, as multiple forms of violence circulate transnationally. Families are divided across space and over time, dispossessed of home and deunified by the U.S.-Mexico border. The absences of deportation are disorienting, dislocating people from lives once lived.

This is dis/order of a new magnitude: the state attempts to create order in the face of chaos, a chaos that, paradoxically, the state itself creates. The "state of exception"[1] becomes the norm: that is, as crisis becomes routine, the exceptional becomes everyday, and chaos may become the only order one knows. The roots of deportation's chaos—this uncertainty of time, place, family, and categories—can be found in the profound inhospitality the nation extends to others. Undocumented migrants, deportees, and their loved ones, regardless of status, must navigate the dehumanization that occurs across a spectrum of formal and informal processes, from unjust shaming[2] to practices designed by immigration authorities to disorient and intimidate. When the state denies or "undoes" presence—and removes or de facto removes migrants and their family members—it directly "unmakes" kin and "undoes" membership in the nation and beyond. The combined formal and informal implementation of removal is the basis of a new system of exclusion in the twenty-first century.

Finally, the making of "displaceable" subjects results in absences and disappearances of different kinds that are experienced by a wide range of migrants and their families. Migrants resist the many forms and tactics of disappearance they encounter: individual and collective agency articulated through a range of acts—from formal protests and informal demonstrations of resistance to preemptively "disappearing" from daily life in the United States—might even be perceived as a direct challenge to the state's banishment of foreign nationals. Yet despite the persistence of family ties and relatedness in the face of migration and removal, the contingency of citizenship is felt widely. As migrants move by force and by will across international boundaries, there is possibility but especially precarity. Alienation and eroded citizenship reflect potentiality foreclosed.

The book opened with Artemio's deportation, a forced movement from north to south that was, like all deportations—albeit to varying degrees—chaotic and disorienting. Returning to the United States after a year of fieldwork in Mexico, during a border crossing from south to north, I also witnessed a glimpse of the chaos of transnational movement and restricted border crossings. Upon deplaning in Los Angeles after a direct flight from Zacatecas, passengers were greeted by confusion and disorder. The experience made me recall Artemio's description of that terrifying night: this was a climate that, while distinct from the setting of Artemio's deportation in significant ways, was similarly framed by chaos and fear. As we walked off the plane, the jetway was blocked by multiple ICE agents and several service dogs barking and jumping as people tried to make their way past them through the narrow passage. It was visibly intimating and disorienting for those on the flight, and, after more than a decade of traveling between Mexico and the United States and having never experienced anything comparable, it seemed to me that the intensity of border control and the state's attempt to restrict movement had reached a point that is momentous. Of course, this border crossing was far from the most violent of passages, but it signaled the everyday chaos that has come to define migration and return.

A TRANSNATIONAL RETURN

One aspect seems certain for all migrants affected by deportation: future trajectories will be linked to ongoing transnationalism in its many forms.[3] As I concluded my previous book, *Intimate Migrations,* I speculated that the lives of Mexican migrants would continue to be shaped by what the anthropologist Roger Rouse has called a "chronic, contradictory transnationalism."[4] This seems to be even more certain in the context of deportation. As I saw again and again, ties between both countries are nearly certain, and "going" and "coming" between Mexico and the United States can be difficult to disentangle. Much of the research about Mexican migration to the United States, including my own, has considered movement from a transnational perspective,[5] but there has not yet been comparable ethnographic, binational, and longitudinal study of deportation and forced return between the two countries, largely because this is a story that is still unfolding.

Although the state deports foreign nationals with a sense of finality, such removals are fundamentally linked to migration and should therefore be considered within a transnational frame.[6] Ties to both countries, in/formal membership in either place, and family relationships that transcend any one nation certainly shape the experiences of those who go back. It may seem counterintuitive to interpret deportation as inevitably transnational. From the standpoint of the state enacting the removal, deportation is simply expulsion: individuals are sent away through the ostensibly permanent act of removal. But this perspective can obscure or even make invisible the inherently transnational dimensions of deportation and return. The directionality of deportation is assumed to be predictable: a one-way flow of movement through which the state sends foreign nationals "back." Still, as people are forcibly removed from the nation, migrate according to previous and emergent paths, and/or are trapped within a nation, be it Mexico or the United States, the explicitly transnational character of deportation's mobilities and even immobilities comes into relief.

In an age of deportation, directionality is certainly mixed up, evidenced in migrants' use of the different terms of location interchangeably: "here" and "there," "migrating" and "staying," "going" and "coming." Repeatedly during interviews about deportation, people in Mexico would say "here" to refer to the United States or "there" to refer to Mexico, even as we spoke south of the border. They would quickly catch themselves and clarify their words, but even this supposed slip seems to signal a notable shift in transnational movement. New migrations may be unexpectedly from the global north to the global south, or migration can (again) take place from the global south to the global north but within new parameters, with far more risk, and with the potential for even more dangerous consequences. Deportation relies on actual and symbolic mobilities and connections to more than one country, as foreign nationals are removed from one place and sent to another. The geographies of return are both supported by and challenge previous articulations of transnationalism.

On the one hand, these are reversed transnational flows that challenge or question the supposed predictability of directionality and generational patterns thought to be part of migration. The state's removal of individuals from its territory to outside the borders of the nation does indeed disrupt certain suppositions in migration studies, as movement from north to south crisscrosses historical and contemporary migrations. Forced return can confound models and understandings of movement that have long guided the work of migration studies scholars. In much of this research, migration is expected to follow certain trajectories driven by structural pressures, economic realities, and "rational" decisions: movement is anticipated from south to north, from "developing" to "developed" countries, from rural to urban, from places with fewer opportunities to those with more. In this analysis, transnational ties are likely to link sending and receiving destinations, as those in receiving communities stay connected to loved ones "at home." Although there are exceptions to predictive frameworks, much of the interdisciplinary migration research begins with these assumptions.

On the other hand, is this a form of transnationality that is altogether new? Are returns in fact inversions or reverse migrations? Certainly, through deportation, movement is increasingly from north to south, from "developed" to "developing" countries, from urban to rural, and from places with ample opportunities to towns with few or none. Yet despite these reversals, there are important parallels between the transnational movement of migration and that of deportation. Will the transnational dimensions of ritual, remittances, political involvement, religion, and social spheres take on familiar transnational forms? When people return after return, or return again, will it result in similar ties but now with the United States as home nation? For example, one can imagine U.S. citizen children in Mexico going "back" north to study or deportees maintaining meaningful ties with loved ones at home—now the United States—through telephone calls, photographs, or gift exchange across borders.

Still, in many ways this is transnationalism of a new kind and character. Although movement crosses transnational borders, the fluidity implicit in transnational frames is upset by the forced mobility and resulting immobility of deportation. This is transnationalism in a fragmented form, transnationality that is disrupted even as it is enacted. The supposed voluntary migrations of family members of those deported and reterritorialization of family is far from the ideal for kin groups, so this, too, captures an interrupted yet persistent form of transnationality. Deportation and its accompanying migrations disrupt but also expand understandings of transnational movement, as family life itself is both upended and reconfigured across borders. Here, transnationalism can include forced transnationalism, unexpected returns, returns after return, and even a kind of transnational immobility through which one can be stuck on either side of the border with aims to cross north or south at some point in the future.

Finally, in addition to the transnationality of geography and future trajectories, those who are deported and those who are affected by deportation will inevitably transcend national boundaries in terms of identity and membership, both that which is constructed and imagined by the self and that which is imposed formally by the state. Transnational lives produce identities marked by loyalty, affiliation, and belonging linked to more than one place, and those affected by deportation are likely to be transnational subjects who are members of more than one nation-state, even if not formally or "legally" recognized as such. Although some researchers have argued that transnationalism signals a weakening of the state,[7] or even a celebration of ways that borders are transcended, globalization "is not only compatible with statehood; it has actually fueled the desire for it."[8] Transnationalism underscores vulnerabilities of (and due to) state power but especially reformulations of it.[9] Transnational encounters are perhaps best understood as clashes or "friction,"[10] exchanges laden with "growing inequality"[11] and marginalization. How is the state served by both of these forms of cross-border movement—migration and return?

Against a backdrop of ongoing transnational movement, the state emerges as both durable and not completely so, but deportation especially reveals the dark elements of state power. Current and emergent forms of state control, restrictive immigration policies, a tightening of the border, and the criminalization of others—what Didier Fassin calls "the policiarization of immigration"[12]—are arguably even more damaging than state actions that came before. One primary difference: today's transnational forms, those that stem from state removals, are not cross-border connections that are likely to hold promise for transformation. Instead, these are ties better analyzed with circumspection, linkages that transcend national boundaries despite danger, violence, and increasing government action. Certainly, deportation and removal are intertwined with past and future transnational flows, but rather than demonstrating an abundance of transnational connections removal shows glimpses of transnational ties that are maintained despite the state's erosion of human connections and the overt dismantling of family life.

So, in this context of continuing transnationality, how are we to make sense of deportation and return? Is deportation return migration, exile, displacement, homecoming? As I have outlined, a defining characteristic of return is that it is shifting, chaotic, and disorienting, so such categorization—like the state's slippery categorization of transnational subjects—may be futile. Emergent transnational movement further muddles the line between going and coming, migration and return. Return also brings about shifting notions of "home" and new ideas of what constitutes "sending" and "receiving" communities. Here, home may be the origin or the destination, or home may be situated in multiple places. Revisiting scholarly considerations of transnational movement can reveal insights about removal and return but can also guide the recalibration of transnational theories themselves. However, in the end, whether the people affected by deportation are most fittingly understood as transmigrants, exiles, refugees, deportees, or nomads matters less than the experiences of dispossession, alienation, and dehumanization that they share.

BE/COMING

One day Lucía invited me over for a visit. She said that she had been thinking about my research and had some reflections that might be helpful.[13] Sitting next to a shrine to the Virgin of Guadalupe, Lucía told me how much she missed the United States—her home for so many years. She said that, although she never imagined she would, she found herself nostalgic about life in *el norte* and even *los bolillos* (slang for white U.S. citizens, lit., "white sandwich rolls"). She recalled her first weeks in a community outside of Dallas, Texas: "It was awful . . . I missed Mexico so! I couldn't imagine creating a life for our family there. But that's exactly what happened. Over time we became comfortable there. Our children studied, made friends—my youngest son was born there. It became our home."

The shrine was colorful: under the Virgin were several photographs framed by bright flowers. Lucía had placed these devotional objects in her home to protect family members still in the United States. She pointed to the photos of her adult children living north of the border, two sons and a daughter. They continued to live without documents in Texas, and after the struggles of their father, Carlos—especially the shame of weeks of detention—Lucía worried every day about the safety of her children. She admitted that it was a risk for them to continue to live there, but, like their sister, Marisol, they were—in every way except for the papers—from the United States.

Lucía had also included photographs of her grandchildren in the shrine. She told me how proud of them she was. Although her grandchildren are all U.S. citizens, she feared for their safety as well. She wondered, what would happen if their parents, her children, were detained by *la migra*? Would they lose custody of their beloved children? Lucía did not know when or even if she would see her grandchildren again, although she was hopeful that their U.S. citizenship will enable them to travel to Mexico when they are older. Lucía told me that she prayed each day for her family in the United States and hoped that they would continue to be safe.

As we spoke over the noise of a construction project taking place at the back of the house—they were installing a bathroom—Lucía described the temporal aspects of the family's return: "We have had to start over . . . we're like newlyweds with nothing. When I left Mexico years ago, we didn't plan to return. We are starting from the beginning this time." Echoing Mariela and so many others who had spoken with me about deportation and return, Lucía described the unpredictability of her and her family's future. "¿Quién sabe?," she asked. She went on: "My husband says he will never return, but I will go if I need to. There hasn't been any rain! If we aren't able to plant, there will be no bean harvest. How can we survive like this? Yes, if I must, I will go. I don't know how, but I will go."

She said that she did not know if she would continue to have the "luck" she had had the previous times she had crossed with a coyote. It was different then, she explained. "It is hard to know . . . I wonder if the next time I cross it will not be so easy. I crossed twice without problems, but one never knows what will happen." Even as Lucía and Carlos made arrangements for their future in Mexico—cleaning out their home that had been empty for more than a decade, building a bathroom, buying a refrigerator with remittances from their children, requesting a telephone line—they were both aware that the future was unpredictable.

Those who return or "come back" to Mexico following deportation must also in a sense "become" someone new, as they recraft futures and selves in significant ways. *Coming,* then, leads to *becoming.* Of course, reinventions of oneself and one's future is part of all human experience, but like the involuntary movement that precipitated migrants' returns, these are forced reinventions. Coming back or even coming for the first time ushers in multiple experiences of becoming, changes that may or may not have a place in one's own imaginings for the future. Movement across geographic landscapes also forces unexpected shifts in time, as becoming creates unfamiliar and unexpected selves, trajectories, and lives. The narratives of deportees and those close to them repeatedly focus on this uncertainty, impermanence, and unpredictability of future events, lives, locations, and selves.

As I have shown throughout the book, individual and family trajectories after deportation can be traced across spatial and temporal scales. Space, and especially the state's control of movement across territory, shapes this process of "becoming."[14] As the cultural geographer David Harvey reminds us, "Symbolic orderings of space and time provide a framework for experience through which we learn who or what we are in society."[15] Narratives of temporalities are disrupted as deportees and their families scramble to situate lives thrown into the past, frozen in the present, or blocked from a once-imagined future. For deportees and their family members, the state's forced reorganization of space and time are central, defining and restricting the "time horizon"[16] of selfhood.

Although all understandings of the future include some uncertainty, through deportation the "intertwining of categorizations of time and certainty"[17] quickly unravels. Given "the darkness of this time"[18] for those who cross borders without authorization, the future of any one migrant and undocumented migrants more generally in the United States is indeed uncertain. Migrants move into the future by reconnecting to their past, a shift back in time as they simultaneously look forward and try to imagine a new life: "Life histories are histories of becoming, and categories can sometimes act to freeze that process of becoming."[19] Such restrictions are the few certainties amid the uncertainty of deportation.

Yet when everything falls apart trajectories are, by necessity, rewritten. As they recast and reimagine the future, deportees and their family members engage in the production of novel selves. Recrafted—or repeatedly crafted—selves are certainly recognizable to all of us,[20] but deportation arguably speeds up this process, intensifies it, and shapes or even limits outcomes in unfamiliar ways. As scholars have shown, in diverse contexts of transition, future possibilities range from profound suffering to stagnation to transformation. In one's undoing, or, as in the case of deportation, the experience of being "undone" by others, there is also possibility: lives and selves are potentially, or by necessity, redone through the "constitutive possibility of becoming otherwise."[21] People pick up the pieces and put lives back together, reconceptualizing time and recasting futures, fashioning something new to the extent that they are able.

Giorgio Agamben describes "potentialities" as a concept that "has never ceased to function in the life and history of humanity."[22] Of course, "potentialities" may hold both despair and possibility. In a sense, "all potentiality is impotentiality," a combination of what one can and cannot do.[23] There is the possibility for events and futures to be actualized but also the "potential not to pass into actuality."[24] Possibilities *and* impossibilities and potentialities *and* impotentialities create a narrative of who we are that may deny ourselves "at the same time that it holds out . . . promise."[25] There is a simultaneity to potentiality, on the one hand, and, on the other, the material and emotional limitations that those affected by deportation must negotiate. Undoing can be destructive, but paradoxically it can also produce innovations.

Although migrants repeatedly look to the potential for making a future and remaking family life in the context of forced return, such agency and opportunity is available only in a very constrained sense. The anthropologist Nathalie Peutz found that after deportation Somalis were "required to narrow their identity, not broaden it."[26] This is the bind of "return" and disrupted temporalities: as time moves forward and back, is compressed and inverted, it requires recalibration. However, with "possibilities now diminished" through deportation,[27] the experience of *becoming* narrows. Life trajectories are framed by potentiality for all of us, but for those who have been deported or affected by the deportation of others such reinventions can be limited. Rocks get in the way.

But, and there always seems to be a "but" in the process of becoming—yet another unforeseen turn or development—there is resiliency despite despair. Even in the darkest moments of deportation, becoming is expressed as possibility: a hope for something else, the desire for something more, a glimpse of an alternative path. As tenuous as the relationship is, Alma will continue to try to form a bond with her granddaughter "through photos" to the extent that she can. Families such as Carlos and Lucía's will be remade, in Mexico or in the United States, depending on the possibilities available to them at any given time. Livelihoods will be redirected, such as how Artemio went back to farming or Federico embarked on a new career trajectory after return. As Marisol adjusts to a likely future in Mexico, life moves on. And while such potentialities are not exactly hopeful, or not what they likely could have been, they do demonstrate human connections and creativity in even the most challenging circumstances. Still, when "possibility is a necessity,"[28] these are potentialities not fully realized, as those affected by deportation depart down paths to partial or limited futures.

Recasting Futures and Selves

Here, I provide updates about some of the individuals and families described throughout the book but with the caveat that trajectories are changing and being rewritten each day. Several of those who were deported have moved transnationally or stayed in Mexico while others have moved. Still others are transnationally stuck, unable to move, but immobile within an undeniable transnational frame. The reinventions of self that migrants express reveal possibilities and potentiality but also impossibilities and narrowed futures.

. . .

Artemio has decided to stay in Mexico for now. He has returned to a life of farming, and he described it as a fairly smooth transition. The horrors of his deportation and return are still vivid at times, but as each day passes the United States and his memories of life there become more distant. For Artemio, investment in the United States was not as deep as that for many migrants. His wife and children never joined him there, his everyday life centered on work, and there was a transience that shaped his experience. It did not feel like home, and in the end, forcibly expelled from the nation, it was not a place he could call his own. Still, although Artemio was traumatized by his deportation and does not intend to return anytime soon, it is difficult to predict the decisions he might make, or be compelled to make, in the future.

· · ·

Rodrigo and Teresa, removed while following the law, underwent expedited removal—a process by which U.S. Border Patrol agents serve as law enforcement, judge, and jury. Rodrigo and Teresa were deported in a matter of hours but with lasting effects. Both told me that, for now, they will stay in Mexico. They are fortunate to have many family members in the United States who can send remittances if farming does not go well. They have a kind of transnational support that mirrors previous cross-border ties, although in their case support goes to those "sent back" rather than to those "left behind" as is typically the case with migration.

And, in an unexpected development, Rodrigo and Teresa's family has now experienced yet another deportation. During one of my field research trips to their town, I was surprised to learn that their son, Isaac, had also been deported. Isaac told me that he had gone with an uncle to the United States when he was just fourteen years old. Because he was young, his uncle insisted that he study, so he attended a year of middle school and two years of high school, more education than he likely would have received had he not migrated. Then, as a teenager, he started working for a landscaping company in Albuquerque. He worked with the same company for nearly a decade; they were so pleased with his performance that they promoted him to a managerial position and moved him to an office in southern New Mexico.

Isaac described that new town and community as "strange." Although he was an undocumented migrant, he had frequent interactions with ICE agents—at the market, passing them on the highway, and even maintaining their yards. He was there for just over a year before he was deported. Isaac explained that one of his employees frequently showed up late and did not seem dedicated to his job. When Isaac mentioned this to one of the owners, his subordinate became disgruntled and called *la migra*. One day after Isaac arrived home, federal agents apprehended him, his wife, and a coworker. They were transported in a large bus, with only the three of them inside, to the border and immediately deported with no money or belongings. As Isaac described the timeline of his migration and deportation during our interview, he realized that, now in his late twenties, he had spent more than half of his life living north of the border. Just as migration can carry across generations, so, too, can deportation. Through a kind of second-generation deportation, multiple generations of Rodrigo and Teresa's family are now in Mexico once more.

. . .

Fátima and David had spoken with me several times about what it was like to live with deportability in their everyday lives, so it was especially troubling when they faced the very concrete possibility of removal. Several years after we first met, I received a phone call from their adult daughter, Bea. She was clearly distressed, talking very quickly about what had transpired. The previous summer, Bea had married a U.S. citizen and become a permanent resident. Then, based on advice they received from a legal aid clinic, Fátima, David, and Bea's younger brother, Mateo, filed to change their status through Bea. They were told by the immigrant advocacy organization that their case was strong and that—because they were law-abiding members of the community—the application process would be straightforward. Based on this information and wanting very much to have formally recognized status in the United States, they filed the necessary paperwork and paid the required fees.

Shortly after appearing at U.S. Citizenship and Immigration Services for a scheduled interview, however, they received a letter that changed their course indefinitely. The letter stated that because Fátima and David had overstayed a tourist visa and had resided in the United States without authorization for many years their application had been denied. The USCIS agent working on their case advised them that they had violated several laws, that there was no opportunity for appeal, and that they should leave the country immediately or risk being deported. Their case, too, represents the erratic and unpredictable character of deportation. While David and Fátima were not directly affected by several rounds of raids in their community, later, while aiming to follow the law, their fears were realized. Given that the risk of deportation is greater today, they found themselves even more vulnerable than they had previously imagined possible.

After more than a decade of residence in the United States, and because they and all their children now have lives firmly rooted in the country, Fátima and David do not consider return to Mexico a viable option. "I am so scared," explained Bea. "I wonder if my parents should go back to Mexico, but my mother refuses. She says she won't leave her children behind. You know how she is—she has made up her mind, and I don't think she will change it." Shortly after our conversation, the family met with an immigration attorney whose advice was to stay in the United States for the time being since a removal order had not (yet) been officially issued. So the family continues to live north of the border but with the constant threat that several family members could be deported at any time.

. . .

Each time I visited with Federico and his family he repeated how much he hoped that he and Gaby would be able to return to the United States. He told me that they would only do so, however, if they were able to find a way to go "home" within the boundaries of the law. For some time after I returned to the United States following fieldwork, I would receive regular emails from Federico inquiring about the possibility of a pardon or an appeal. "Perhaps there is another way to receive permission to enter the country?," he would ask. I wrote to several immigration attorneys I knew and shared the details of the case, but little came of it. All the attorneys had the same read on Federico and Gaby's situation: authorized return after deportation is nearly impossible. Any chance of documented return was extremely unlikely.

Federico's emails about a possible pardon tapered off. I also kept in touch with his daughters, whose lives seemed increasingly rooted in the United States. His older daughter made several trips to Mexico, so Federico and Gaby were able to meet their first grandchild. For this they are very grateful. Federico and Gaby reluctantly remain in Mexico even as they continue to search for a way to one day return to the United States through "legal" channels. The last time I heard from Federico, he again asked about paths to changing his status: Perhaps an attorney could find a way? Wouldn't a pardon be possible? Was there any way to "fix" the situation and ultimately reverse the deportation?

. . .

When I last spoke with Carlos and Lucía, Carlos was adamant that he would stay in Mexico, although the family's ties to the United States are strong. Currently, three of Carlos and Lucía's children are living in Mexico, and the three eldest are in the United States. Carlos has returned to his life as a farmer, and Lucía is again, hesitantly, taking on the responsibilities of a full-time homemaker—identities they thought they had left behind when they first migrated to the United States. Lucía had told me that she would be willing to go north if they needed the money, creating a possible inversion in the gendered dynamics of migration. Or, Lucía said, perhaps their thirteen-year-old son, Eduardo, would leave in a couple of years as an undocumented labor migrant just as his father had done decades before.

Carlos and Lucía also expect that their young son, Nico, a U.S. citizen, will some day return to "his country." Still, after a childhood in Mexico following his father's deportation from his nation of origin, Nico is likely to have a liminal status in both the United States and Mexico. Certainly, a return north will be far more straightforward for Nico as a U.S. citizen than for his siblings and parents, who do not have authorized status in the United States. But after his de facto deportation and years of living a form of exile in Mexico, Nico's membership and place in the nation will likely be compromised, far from what it could have been.

Carlos and Lucía have attempted to step back into life in Mexico, yet the homecoming has not been smooth. As Lucía stood next to the garden that she has built since her return, surrounded by cages of small songbirds, she described feeling closed in, trapped by the deportation of her husband: "There, in the north, our life was good . . . here, we seem to have only bad luck. We can't get ahead, we can barely get by." Lucía told me that she is seriously contemplating a return to the United States without Carlos. She admits that it would be difficult, but if she has to, she will go north again—even if she must do so alone.

• • •

Dina and Sergio, who described the details of violence in their home community, had told me that after two years apart when Sergio was in the United States, they were unlikely to divide the family again through migration. This was still their feeling when we last spoke. The family was together in Mexico without immediate plans to travel to the United States. Dina said she would be interested in going north as a family to visit her sisters in Texas—but only if they are able to get tourist visas. She believes it would be a good experience for her daughters to be in the United States for several months, learning English and spending time with family members there. Dina thought that perhaps the violence in the region had waned a bit, but it was hard to know. After all, she explained, many of the violent acts go unreported, uninvestigated, and unacknowledged. For now, they will all stay in Mexico, but like most people I interviewed, Dina and Sergio were uncertain about what the future would bring.

. . .

Just before I left Mexico, Emy invited me over to visit. She was feeling upbeat, even hopeful, she said. She was focused on the festivities for Cora's upcoming *quinceañera* and the many family members from the United States who were likely to make the trip south for it. Cora joined us in the living room and said that she, too, was looking forward to the event, although she had just spoken with her best friend and learned that she would not be able to attend the party after all. Her parents were nervous about having a teenager travel on her own, let alone to a place they thought was "dangerous" and "filled with *narcos*." Cora continued to miss the United States and to strategize a return. "Maybe I could go back with you!," she said, glancing at her mother. Emy laughed but shook her head definitively.

Emy said she was most looking forward to her husband Manuel's return for the birthday celebration and the chance to see him again after nearly a year apart. Cora admitted that she, too, was eager to have the family living in one place, even if she would rather it be in the United States. Because Manuel is undocumented, it will be a risk to return south because another return north would certainly be a challenge. Still, Emy thought it was time to reevaluate the family's living arrangements. She explained that a return to the United States—the children (again) with a coyote and Emy and Manuel "*por el desierto* [through the desert]"—was likely, "that is, if they don't detain me again." I asked what the family would do if they choose, or are forced, to stay in Mexico. Sighing, Emy continued, "I don't know, I really don't know. We are more used to being here now, and I am comfortable, but it isn't the same as it is in the north. We don't have anything here—no money for food, no work, nothing."

Emy told me that she would prefer to return again to the United States but that plans were uncertain, and she could not be sure what would happen next. Then, just a few months after I had returned to the United States, I received an unexpected phone call from Emy. She and Manuel and all the children were again in the United States. The family was reunited, for now. She described the border crossing as a difficult one and admitted that she had been terrified about the possibility of being apprehended a second time. Still, even with the many risks involved in crossing the border and the high stakes of her reentry after deportation, Emy felt a certain security "returning" to the United States, a place that, like her U.S. citizen children, she identifies as home. As our conversation came to a close, she passed the phone to Cora so that we could chat. Cora said she was still "bored"—primarily because her cell phone had just stopped functioning—but it was so much better to be "back home" and to reconnect with friends again. She related one particular challenge: the year in Mexico had put her behind in her studies, and, embarrassingly, she had to be held back in school. Now one of the oldest students in her class, Cora is out of place once more.

· · ·

Tomás was matter of fact about the deportation and where it was likely to lead him. Yes, he said, he hoped to return to the United States at some point in the future, but it would not be Texas this time. If he goes north again, California will be the likely destination, primarily because life was "easier" for him there. "Even though you were living above the restaurant and working all the time?," I asked. He shrugged and smiled. "Well, I didn't get deported from California." He was making very little money in Mexico, just enough to get by. He was working on his family's land but also taking on occasional work in other families' fields, primarily migrant families with no adult men living in Mexico.

Planting and harvesting had previously been done by migrant men during seasonal returns, but now deportees and other returnees were available for hire. Families were appreciative of the opportunity to continue growing beans, but as more migrants were deported, the need for farmhands was diminishing. Tomás told me he would keep accepting work until it was no longer available. At that point, perhaps he would reconsider migration. He admitted that as time passed the details of the deportation were fading, so he might be willing to again migrate. He said that, of course, he hoped to someday meet his daughter in person but that realistically the relationship with his former partner, Layci, was probably unsalvageable. "But," he shrugged, "who knows?"

· · ·

During a particularly memorable conversation with Marisol in Mexico, she had shown me one of the few tangible objects she had from her childhood in the United States: when she learned that she would be going back to Mexico and in anticipation of the estrangement she would soon embark on, Marisol decided to create a scrapbook, a collection of memories, before she left. As Marisol turned the pages, she pointed out significant moments. Under a faded photograph of her first communion she had written, "Me when I was little." There was a Polaroid taken by her fourth-grade teacher with some of her friends in elementary school, the children of immigrants from different parts of the world with whom she so closely identified. The scrapbook was also filled with photos of her siblings and friends who were still living in the United States. As she turned the pages, she described memories of another time, another life.

On the last page, Marisol had included a saying that she told me she especially liked: "The sum of all your attitudes and thoughts comprises your overall attitude." She explained that she has had to make the best of her situation. Although she is eager to return to the United States, her undocumented status will make it extremely difficult to do so. Marisol left the country just before DACA was announced and implemented, so this option is not available to her. In another unpredictable turn, had she stayed in the United States, she likely would have qualified and successfully deferred a removal order. Now, however, it is uncertain when or even if she will again be in the country where she grew up.

Marisol recounted that she was unhappy after she first arrived in Mexico, that she immediately started to make plans to return to the United States: "My brothers were going to pay for a coyote, but my parents didn't want me to leave. It was very difficult when we were apart. In the end, they didn't want me to go, and that made me reconsider, too. I decided I would rather be here with my parents than be there without them." Marisol wants to respect her parents' wishes to have her in Mexico, so for now she will stay. As she closed the scrapbook, I asked what she imagined her future will be, what she hoped it would be. She replied, "I hope I can improve our lives—my family's future and mine."

. . .

During my research, Tito and Amanda had spoken with me about Mexico's "lawlessness" but also the risk of "the law" in the United States. Both naturalized U.S. citizens whose children also have U.S. citizenship, Tito and Amanda do not live with the threat of deportation or the likelihood of an unexpected return to Mexico. Still, through family ties, they worry about deportability and deportation constantly, wondering what might happen to their siblings, nieces and nephews, aunts and uncles. They are also concerned about Amanda's mother, who has U.S.

permanent residency and travels back and forth frequently but must do so in a context of violence and insecurity.

Several of Tito and Amanda's nieces and nephews are U.S. citizens with undocumented migrant parents. Amanda said she has tried to persuade two of her sisters to draw up legal documents granting custody to Amanda and Tito should "anything happen." "I told them that they should write letters giving permission for us to take the children if they are detained or deported." Amanda admitted that this was unpleasant to think about and would be a far from ideal arrangement, but it seemed a way to ensure limited security, what Amanda described as the best way "to protect their U.S. citizen children."

. . .

Jasmin and Nacho and their young children continue to live in Texas despite Nacho's "disappearance" after he was supposed to leave the United States. Jasmin confirmed that they do indeed fear Nacho's potential deportation, but given limited options, the risk of deportation that they currently live with is preferable to having their family divided and being apart for a decade. For now, they can be together, and then, they hope, they will be formally "reunited" when the ten years required by the government have elapsed.

Nacho made a phantom return to Mexico, through which he has, he hopes, gone on record as having abided by the U.S. government's order. In several years he plans to make yet another phantom return, this time to the United States. When Nacho vanished, he disappeared from a formally recognized existence. In a sense, Nacho went from being undocumented to hyperdocumented, once paperwork was filed by Jasmin, and back again. In another inversion caused by the chaos of potential deportation, Jasmin can continue to "return" with her children to a place none of them are from, while her husband—ostensibly in Mexico—is "trapped" or unable to leave the United States if he is to continue to be with his family.

. . .

After Jaime arrived in his hometown in Mexico, his absence from the United States lingered. The long-distance relationship with his girlfriend was challenging, he was not able to have much contact with his friends, and he missed his family tremendously. "My cousins ask me, 'Do you want to go back?,' and I say, 'Yeah, 'cause I am not used to being here.' And I ask them, 'Would you like to go over there?' And they say, 'Not really . . . I'm better off here.' I tell them, 'I understand your point of view, but you have to understand mine, because I lived over there and I got used to it and I like it over there.'"

This logic made sense for Jaime, but it also resonates with the many others who are affected by deportation. And so it was that after just a few months in Mexico, Jaime's absence was felt once more. Jaime told me that he was unhappy: he missed his family, could not "get used" to being in Mexico, and did not, he felt, fit in. So Jaime went "home," back to the United States and back to the only life he had ever really known. His border crossing was taxing—he and the coyote were separated, and he was on his own for a stretch—but he made it across safely in the end. Today Jaime is "here" in the United States, yet "not here,"[29] absent even in his presence.[30]

As Jaime moves between work and home, his daily life seems mundane on the surface, yet it is exceptional in terms of the potential outcome should his presence be discovered by U.S. immigration officials. Again out of place and disoriented, Jaime sees his absence from Mexico and from formal belonging in the United States—even with its profound risks—as the most certain and secure status he can have. Yet the power of the state and the fragility of his "place" in this country have created another disappearance, this time from Mexico. Jaime reappeared in the United States but only in a limited way. His status as a returned deportee is on the margins of "illegality" itself, overshadowing and limiting potential future plans for education, work, and family. As he tries to recast his place in the nation, Jaime's movement through space and time is limited, blocked, thwarted. And as he imagines a life yet-to-come, Jaime has tenuous membership in two nations and feels the burden of not fully belonging—and not fully returning—wherever he goes.

Future Returns

After Jaime went back to the United States to reunite with his parents and siblings, the family again felt the fallout of deportation. In a tragic turn of events, Jaime's father was deported shortly after Jaime returned to his parents' home. It was hard for family members to imagine that after such a brief time together they were again forced to live apart, with Jaime's father, mother, and younger sister, a middle school student, living, ironically, in the very town in Mexico that Jaime had left to reunite with family after such a lonely time there without them. Jaime's deportation and return followed by his return to the United States was then followed by his father's deportation and his mother's and sister's return to Mexico. Abruptly, Jaime and his family were forced to launch a new stage of migration and return, as family members were returned south unexpectedly and moved north and south in response to it but in patterns that further divided the family as they were displaced in various locations.

Multiple removals within families represent a curious development in U.S.-Mexico transnationality: second-generation or multigenerational deportation. Removal and return across generations can be experienced by both older and younger kin, as demonstrated by Jaime's deportation followed by his father's and Rodrigo's deportation followed by his son's. Such generations of deportation underscore the unpredictability of transnational movement after deportation and yet the certainty of its continuation: a new era of increased deportation is ushering in new generations of migration and return. These multiple forms of transnational movement, in uncertain directions and according to unpredictable time frames, signal unexpected patterns of state action and transborder movement. Of course, multiple generations of deportees and family members transcending the border is quite different from the transnationalism of previous decades of migration, as migrants have even fewer possibilities for circular migration and face unprecedented risk, violence, and legal sanctions.

So what does the future hold for those who are deported and those around them? What forms are future migrations likely to take? How might shifts in directionality create migrations that are entirely new? What happens when "return" means going back to the place from which one was expelled, when the United States again becomes the destination but now as the place where one returns? How is this different from previous generations of migration to the United States or even decades of seasonal, circular migration? After deportation, deportees such as Jaime and Emy will again return to the United States. Expelled from the country, many deportees describe the finality of return, and yet deportation can be a temporary state. Those connected to deportees and deportees themselves will return but with much higher stakes and even more uncertain futures. David had told me that such returns are likely after deportation: "Although it is very difficult to return again to this country after deportation, there are still many people who do so."

Future migrations and returns, such as "the new American diaspora"[31] that comes out of deportation, will be important to follow and research as they unfold. Although the future trajectories of deportees and migrants are vague and unclear, forced return to Mexico does and will continue to result in migrants' "return migration" to the United States. There is an unpredictability in deportation—of place and directionality, with migrants going and coming, staying and stuck—but curiously a kind of predictability as well in that ongoing ties to the United States are inevitable. Even if future migrations are not realized, at the very least deportees will depend on the remittances of family members living in the United States. Agricultural hardship in home communities, a global economic crisis, increasing violence throughout Mexico, the need for support from remittances, and, significantly, ongoing demand for unauthorized labor in the United States drive such future migrations and "returns" north.

Removal and its aftermath presents a void, a vacuum, and yet it is an uncertainty that is concrete and palpable. Deportees are not alone as they consider limited options; in some respects, all undocumented migrants face a narrowing future. Although hope for comprehensive immigration reform and possibly amnesty remains, it is overshadowed by the immediacy of increasing deportations and the multiple factors that continue to drive migration from Mexico to the United States. Throughout our conversations Lucía had asked, "What does the future hold?" Her question was much like Mariela's, who wondered, "What are those who are returned going to do?" And, similarly, in an interview with David, as I was gathering my things, he asked, rather abruptly, "So where do we go from here?" His question, to which there is no adequate response, has lingered since he asked it.

BETRAYAL

In the spring of 2015, people gathered in protest in northern Nevada. Members of the community stood in silence while holding signs that had been altered with fluorescent markers: "I am deportable" had been crossed out to instead read, "We are all deportable." The reference to being "deportable" had come from an exchange a few months earlier when a member of the U.S. Congress, Steve King, a Republican from Iowa, tweeted that "a deportable" would be attending the State of the Union Address as the guest of First Lady Michelle Obama. The undocumented youth activist to whom King referred was a DACAmented migrant living in Texas. Immigrant advocates seized the derogatory use of the term *deportable* and aimed to reframe it, empowering all to block future deportations and to strive for comprehensive immigration reform. This was, in part, what motivated protesters on that spring day.

But those at the event were also responding to the fact that Nevada's attorney general, Adam Laxalt, had decided to join a lawsuit brought by the State of Texas. The suit explicitly challenged President Obama's executive action to expand an already implemented program, Deferred Action for Childhood Arrivals, or DACA, and to begin a new one, Deferred Action for Parents of Americans and Lawful Permanent Residents (DAPA). Participants in the protest wrote letters to Laxalt expressing their disappointment in what they saw as a betrayal of the state and its immigrant population. Laxalt is, after all, a member of a family that includes some of the state's most famous immigrants, a family that traces its roots to a man who came to Nevada from Basque Country to work as a sheepherder in the early 1900s.

The majority of today's migrations to Nevada come from a different part of the world than those of Adam Laxalt's ancestors: the state has the highest per capita population of undocumented migrants in the United States, the majority from Mexico and other Latin American countries.[32] However, these migrations that are separated by geography and more than a century are perhaps not so different in character. Current migrants to the United States share much with those from previous generations: all have come to support family, all experience struggle to improve their lives, all hope for a better future. What is notably different in the current moment, however, is the chilly reception and profound inhospitality that migrants face when they arrive, if they arrive safely, at the borders of the nation. Unprecedented immigration control and state-enacted removals put new challenges in newcomers' way.

Just as migrants' individual trajectories are uncertain—marked by an unpredictability that permeates all plans for the future—so, too, is the current political milieu and any possibility for immigration policy reform. I have outlined how uncertainty shapes future migrations and the reinventions of selves; similarly, the nation's course for federal immigration policy remains unclear. As the legal challenge to President Obama's executive action continues, the future of DACA and DAPA is uncertain, the possibility for a federal DREAM Act seems unlikely, and a chance for comprehensive immigration reform has been stalled at every turn, such that instead of asking *when*, some activists now ask *if* such legislation will come to fruition. Meanwhile, successes at the local and state level seem to hold some promise for change: from state ID legislation to permitting lawyers to practice in the United States regardless of citizenship, communities throughout the country are experimenting with their own solutions. However, such practices are tempered by exclusionary local ordinances and vigilante actions to sup-posedly "control" immigration at the grassroots level.

There is profound uncertainty as to what precisely the future holds for migrants, deportees, and their loved ones. Relief for immigrant fam-ilies seems a long way off; security and rights are barely visible. I have had the opportunity to work with migrant communities and immigrant advocacy organizations since the 1990s, and while I have seen some change, far more has stayed the same or become that much more threat-ening. Despite our collective identity as a nation of immigrants and as a free and just country, we do not have policies that ensure membership to all those who do in fact belong. The full reach of deportation is still unfolding: as each day passes, more individuals are deported. And, as my research has shown, through relationships with others, far more are "displaceable" than the millions who have been formally expelled from the United States in recent years. They, too, may experience deporta-tion, albeit in de facto or undocumented form.

Indeed, as the signs that day in Nevada expressed, in a sense we are all deportable. Millions are deported, banished from their nation through both formal and informal channels. Many more than the deported are deportable and displaceable. Many more than the deported must depart. As migrants are forced to leave the United States, children, partners, and other loved ones—undocumented migrants, U.S. citizens, U.S. perma-nent residents, DACAmented migrants, and even deportees themselves—accompany loved ones to unfamiliar or entirely unknown homes. Such movement underscores how the parameters of national belonging are often and perhaps too easily eroded, questioned, invalidated.

Still, we are not *all* deportable. Some deport others. Some create the laws that deport others. Some do not understand or make themselves aware of the laws that shape deportation. Others dispute what the "law" should be. Still others disengage, telling themselves that this very com-plex history and story of immigration is a simple one, easily dismissed as "legal" and "illegal" acts. This is, in fact, a new order of injustice. And, as the protesters clearly communicated that day, we are all com-plicit and we all have a stake in immigration policies. We all have much to lose as people are deported each day. Even one more deportation means that loss and suffering will alter a family and their future lives indefinitely.

The chant of immigrant advocates—"*Ni una más* / Not one more"—presents an alternative path to the deportations that have come to define our nation's immigration policies. There is little hope for fully restoring the lives of the millions who have already been devastated by state removals. With each additional deportation, another family is fragmented, more futures are taken away, countless migrants "disappear" from the country they have called home. As I have argued throughout the book, displaceability means that people can swiftly become displaced, detained, deported, departed, and disappeared. Some are perceived as dispensable or disposable. Others vanish from the country and from meaningful connections to family and community.

The reach of deportation is far and wide. The creation of a "displaceable" class, made up of formal and undocumented citizens, redraws the boundaries of those who are perceived as having an authentic claim to the nation and those who are understood to be outsiders. Until we find a system that works, create comprehensive immigration reform, and combat anti-immigrant sentiment and exclusion, we are all complicit in the chaos, the unpredictability, the upheaval. As millions vanish from lives in this country, we all play a role. Chaos and unpredictability create a form of betrayal—of those without formal U.S. citizenship, of those with de facto U.S. citizenship, and, through relatedness, of those who are U.S. citizens. Paradoxically, by deporting millions from the country, the nation also betrays itself.

At the back of a booklet distributed at an information session for undocumented migrants, there was a small drawing offering hope: a crowd of people are standing in front of the U.S. Capitol, smiling and cheering.[33] A banner reads, "*Reforma Migratoria* [Immigration Reform]—Opportunities for All!" Here, an imagined future of security replaces the chaos, uncertainty, and instability of the present. For now, however, the words of migrants tell another story. As David described it, the temporal frame of deportation and deportability is unending: "Day after day, year after year—the fear is damaging." The narratives of deportees, unauthorized migrants, and U.S. citizens capture the contradictions of deportation, its im/permanence and a persistence—even predictability—of uncertainty. It seems that in a milieu characterized both by a growing number of removals of Mexican nationals from the United States and by the need for ongoing transnational migration, there is uncertainty one can count on.

INVISIBILITY

[handwritten annotation: direct statement of intention to argue]

As I have argued throughout the book, deportation results in disappearances of different kinds: precarity, absence, loss, dispossession. Of course, most deportees do not in fact disappear from the world; they are not "disappeared" by the state in ways that many tragically are in so many settings of conflict and war. Still, although there are significant differences between actual disappearances due to state violence and the disappearances of deportation, such analysis is nonetheless important to include here, above all because the idea of "disappearing" was introduced to me by interlocutors themselves. Again and again, people spoke of loved ones who had vanished, of previous lives that seemed to evaporate, of family connections that were severed indefinitely. If we do not speak of deportation's disappearances, we risk reducing descriptions of unjust and oppressive state action to euphemism. After all, deportation is the state's physical removal, through violence and force, of individuals from the nation.

Even if individuals do not in fact disappear—although significantly some do—deportation can indeed cause people to disappear from the United States, to maintain family ties without any face-to-face interactions, and to never again be seen by countless kin, friends, and community members. Relationships with others that are halted and one's embeddedness in community that is no more are among the most profound losses that people describe. Those deported and those displaced because of deportation vanish from a particular place and from everyday life.[34] Even if they do return to the United States some day, though this is unlikely for most, life circumstances will never again return to what they once were; for many migrants, the past fades or disappears completely. And, although dismissed by those I interviewed as relatively insignificant, even large material possessions disappear as if without a trace, such as automobiles and, most painfully, homes that migrants were forced to walk away from. Finally, among the especially difficult losses is the disappearance of one's homeland. Membership, citizenship, and ties to the nation are notably absent after deportation, vacuity where belonging—even if formally limited—once was.

In most cases, disappearance and absence convert into presence elsewhere, a reappearance in another place and another life. But what is on the other end of the disappearances of deportation? By necessity lives move ahead through reconfigurations, revisions, and reinventions, yet after the upheaval of return settles a bit, reappearances are always accompanied by profound loss. Migrants move the rocks aside, but still they experience immeasurable suffering. Absence does typically convert to presence elsewhere, but do the many losses of deportation ever become gains? As those affected by deportation so thoughtfully told me, no, not really. Chaos and suffering lead to recrafting oneself, creative strategies for the future, and a form of survival, but, without question, deportation results in the disappearance of so much.

Finally, through the disappearances of deportation, it is possible to gauge or track how the nation constructs difference. Simply stated, some people are more at risk of disappearing than others. Whether it is a mass grave of vulnerable potential border crossers, individuals who vanish while attempting to enter the United States,[35] those who are formally "removed" by the state, or the many others who are exiled from the nation as a result of the deportation of others, these are disappearances from a life once known but never fully actualized. Here, alienization and othering can easily become absence, as people in a particular life or reality rapidly slip into another or disappear completely. Through the inequality of the current moment—this tenuous existence for so many—millions of people are at risk of disappearing. Indeed, countless members of the nation already have.

As I conclude the book, I again return to the "ghosts" of deportability and deportation, to the phantom lives removal produces. Barely visible are the outlines of the millions who have been deported, the millions more who have gone with them, and the more than 11 million undocumented migrants,[36] most of them de facto citizens, who continue to live in the shadows in the United States. When individuals are deported and their lives upended, a phantom presence lingers. Similarly, when deportees "return" to the United States—again without authorization but now with stakes that are much higher—their reappearance in the nation is also a kind of disappearance, as they must go "underground"[37] in an effort to recreate a life in the very place they were forced to leave. These concealed experiences can quickly convert into invisible struggles. The aftermath of return in the lives of deportees and their loved ones is for the most part unseen as life trajectories go unrecognized and unrecorded.

• • •

As for Miguel—first held hostage in an apartment in Texas, then apprehended in Nevada, and finally deported from California—one day he simply disappeared. For months I saw him without fail on a particular street corner in Zacatecas, washing cars, smiling and joking with those who passed by. His ties to the United States were in some ways the weakest of the migrants I interviewed: he had been there a very short time, and he did not have any family or community members in the

United States to protect him. He was especially vulnerable in terms of financial resources. And so Miguel was deported. He had struggled to create a life for himself in Mexico once more. He worked long days cleaning the cars of those more privileged than he was. One of his daughters was in elementary school, and for this he was proud. His older daughter, Abril, still grade-school age herself, was not studying. Miguel, not able to do the job alone, needed her to come to work with him. But, he assured me, Abril would return to school when they could again afford the luxury.

And then, one day, without warning or fanfare, Miguel vanished from everyday life. He had told me that he was likely to go back to the United States, this time without a coyote in order to save on expenses. After having been held in an apartment for weeks by those who were supposed to ensure his safe passage, he did not really trust coyotes anyway. He said that he thought he could remember how to cross. "But I hope I can find the way," he added. Perhaps he did not actually disappear from Mexico; maybe he took his car washing business elsewhere, or he and his family might have moved to a larger city in hopes of finding steadier employment. Yet whether he has relocated in Mexico or is en route to the United States or in *el norte* or another destination, his absence persists. I often wonder where Miguel is today. He may have made it back to the United States to work, as he hoped, or, in that violent desert expanse, as he attempted to cross into the United States without a coyote, perhaps something went terribly wrong. Indeed, it already has.

Lost

Hopefully I won't get lost.

—Miguel

In a conversation about my research on deportation, a friend from the city of Zacatecas—an urban Zacatecano—made an observation that has stayed with me as I have witnessed and tried to make sense of migrants' experiences of return and being returned. My friend remarked, almost in passing, that the migrants I work with are *"ciudadanos perdidos,"* or lost citizens, and then he repeated a refrain I have often heard in my research with migrants, typically from migrants themselves: *"No son de aquí ni de allá* [They are from neither here nor there]." When I asked why he chose this specific word—*lost*—to describe his fellow citizens, he replied that return migrants are not fully part of either country, excluded from the United States but not entirely Mexican. "Of course, they are my *paisanos* [fellow nationals]," he explained, "but their lives are very different from mine. It is difficult to know what will become of them."

While this sentiment of being "from neither here nor there" has framed my ongoing research with migrant communities,[1] "lost citizens" is a category of alienation that signals a new global order of injustice. We do not all have equal access to citizenship and membership in particular nations. We do not all have the same chances to move across borders. As the world becomes a more connected place for some, the disconnections, barriers, and spaces of exclusion grow for most. This label "lost citizens," like the many categories explored throughout the book, is shifting and relational. My friend seemed to understand this, identifying with migrants as members of the nation but also recognizing the deep divide of experience that separates them.

So, are deportees, returnees, and their family members in fact "lost citizens"? In the sense that their membership is compromised in the nations in which they live, yes, this is certainly the case. So I wonder if these migrants are lost citizens or rather those who have suffered loss, including a kind of "lost citizenship" or absence of full membership. They have lost, or never had—sometimes even in those nations they consider home—the full right to citizenship. Those affected by return are lost citizens in this sense, or perhaps lost citizens might be more aptly understood as those who lose in an era of global movement. The age of deportation is marked by social injustice and striking inequality as subjects move and do not move—forcibly or not, despite and because of state power—across national boundaries throughout the world.

This notion of lost citizens made me recall how Amanda had once described those affected by deportation: they are, she said, "citizens without rights." Her husband, Tito, explained that for undocumented migrants and those who are deported "*no hay salida*"—in other words, there is no exit, no out, no solution, no end. Tito continued, "There are people who want to be in Mexico but who have to stay in the United States because they are undocumented. And there are people who want to be with family in the United States but cannot because they are undocumented. People are stuck." Those with transnational ties are increasingly trapped in either Mexico or the United States but also "caught"[2] between two countries and constrained by systems of membership that do not account for their undeniably transnational lives. Indeed, those affected by deportation can be slotted into an underclass with no out.

Given this new order of injustice, what are the possibilities for transnational migrants and their families? What will become of those who are deported and those who are de facto deported? What are the effects of establishing an emergent and "permanent underclass"[3] of transnational subjects? Deportation is a form of social abandonment or even social death,[4] the result of what Amanda called "inhumane acts by the government." Removal may include a sort of death of part of one's self caused by suffering by and for people now gone. As people are abandoned by the nation and cast aside from the social body, they disappear: materially or literally from country and community but also in less easily definitive ways and from less measurable forms of participation in a

shared future. Each day, human lives are deemed "precarious,"[5] categorized as less than, marked and made abject, dehumanized beyond recognition by the public. The age of deportation is a time of precarity and
dispossession—of families, of family ties, of membership in kin groups
and nations, and increasingly of citizenship itself.

But not all life is equally precarious. As the philosopher Judith Butler
asks, "Who counts as human? Whose lives count as lives? And finally,
What *makes for a grievable life*?"[6] For Jacques Derrida, mourning
involves speaking of the dead.[7] I wonder how circumstances might
change if mourning could also include speaking of the living—but of
those who are deported, displaced, departed, and/or disappeared. Perhaps the first step in reforming policy is witnessing these multiple disappearances, that is, acknowledging and speaking of the disappeared,
articulating the material, emotional, and social losses of deportation in
order to make visible that which is so often invisible. Mourning can
perhaps reveal a different course,[8] one in which the typically unre-
marked on everyday losses of those affected by deportation and return
might be fully appreciated and addressed as they are brought into view.

As the migrants who are presented in this book have expressed, much
is lost after deportation. Such losses certainly are evident to those who
are deported and their loved ones. But we all experience—or should
bear—the burden of deportation. As we reflect on our nation's history
of immigration, it is clear that we all share in the losses and gains of
transnational migration to some degree. The nation has profited, in
every sense of the word, from immigration and global movement, yet
these contributions are often taken for granted. That this is a country
built and rebuilt by multiple generations of colonized and enslaved peoples and migrant laborers from all parts of the world; that national
identity hinges on the United States as a place for the "tired, poor, hud-
dled masses yearning to breathe free"; that ours is a nation more diverse
than any other in the world—these gains are barely visible at times.
Similarly, the exclusions and losses that accompany our national narrative may be undocumented or rarely considered.

All of us should be unsettled by the chaos of return and what it
means for the nation and local communities. We have choices in the
direction we go or do not go as a nation. We can keep policies and support state actions that result in exclusion, displacement, and expulsion.
Or we might return to or go to a time and place paradoxically characterized by local communities aware of their transnational contexts, a

national body made up of and built by and for a multitude of people from near and far. Homecomings can be devastating or joyful or bittersweet. So far, the losses of deportation are many and painful, but, as those who return well know, the future—however deferred—can still be remade.

Acknowledgments

When I first began research on deportation in 2008, I assumed that political circumstances would change in the coming years. I thought it was likely that by the time this book went to press it would provide a snapshot of another moment, a dark period in our nation's history but one replaced by a reasonable approach to immigration reform that ensured rights to those living in the United States. This has clearly not been the case. Still, I am stunned that so little has changed to improve the lives of immigrants and their families over the past decade. In fact, the climate today is arguably among the most exclusionary in our country's history. The voices of far too many in the collective conversation about immigration express ideas and proposals that are racist, demeaning, violent, and dangerous for us all. I present this work as a counter-narrative to such damaging anti-immigrant sentiment, at what I understand to be a time of crisis for the country as we strive to create a place that might indeed live up to the values expected of a democracy and of a nation of immigrants.

So, with the caveat that I wish there was not such strife and uncertainty to convey, I want to thank the many individuals, organizations, and institutions that made the project a possibility and that supported the endeavor as the book came to fruition. First, although I cannot do so by name, I thank the many people who so thoughtfully participated in my research, especially the families that are the focus of the book—those who have felt the impact of deportation and return in the most devastating ways. I was repeatedly impressed by their candidness, sincerity, and strength. Even in the darkest moments people revealed unexpected resiliency, and I am grateful to the individuals who generously shared their intimate experiences with me.

I appreciate my wonderful editor at the University of California Press, Naomi Schneider, for all of her guidance and support. Naomi and everyone at the Press, including Sheila Berg, Jessica Ling, Ally Power, Rose Vekony, and Will Vincent, were helpful each step of the way. I thank the three external reviewers of the manuscript for their recommendations for strengthening the book and hope that I have incorporated these in a manner true to their intent. A very special thanks to a former student, Gabriela Muñoz, for creating such moving artwork and for sharing it on the cover of the book. I was honored to receive the California Series in Public Anthropology Award and to have this book included in the series alongside the work of colleagues I greatly respect. Thanks to Rob Borofsky for his encouragement and for his many efforts to bring the strengths of anthropology to public audiences. I also appreciate being granted permission to incorporate sections of two previous journal articles in the book: thank you to Jack Rollwagen of The Institute, Inc., and Oxford University Press for doing so.

Institutional, economic, and personal support for the project came in many forms. I am especially indebted to the woman I call Mariela in the book for first encouraging me to pursue research specifically about deportation and to the many families that served as such gracious hosts over the years. A Fulbright–García Robles Fellowship supported a year in Mexico to conduct research focused explicitly on return, fieldwork that laid the foundation for this book. Fellow Fulbrighters were great colleagues, and I appreciate the ongoing collaborations and friendships that came from the experience. The community at the Estudios del Desarrollo at the Universidad Autónoma de Zacatecas (UAZ), my host institution for the Fulbright award, was very welcoming. I am grateful for the physical and intellectual space that UAZ provided, the opportunity to formally and informally discuss my research with faculty and students, and Miguel Moctezuma Longoria's support of my project proposal from its inception. Special thanks to those I met or reconnected with in Mexico, including Jeanette Acosta, Fernando Saúl Alanis Enciso, Carina Alencar, Federico Besserer, Judy Boruchoff, Isabel Cardenas, Mark Davidson, Mónica Díaz, Mark Dunn, Patricia Dunn, Jenny Emery-Davidson, Tory Gavito, Nora Haenn, David Martin, Kate McCormack, Héctor Mendoza, Kim Nolan, Antonio Ramirez, Ethan Sharp, and Audrey Singer.

An American Council of Learned Societies Fellowship generously supported a year of leave for writing, a priceless gift. During the fellowship year, I was fortunate to join the School for Advanced Research (SAR) in Santa Fe, New Mexico, as a visiting research associate. I want to thank everyone at SAR for creating such a rich environment for anthropological inquiry and for the opportunity to connect with an outstanding group of scholars and friends: Rebecca Allahyari, Patricia Baudino, Abby Bigham, Kent Blansett, Philippe Bourgois, Jon Daehnke, Laurie Hart, Laura Holt, Islah Jad, George Karandinos, He Li, Amy Lonetree, Lisa Pacheco, Nicole Taylor, and Jordan Wilson. As a visiting scholar at the Center for the Study of Law and Society at the University of California, Berkeley, School of Law, I continued work on the manuscript and was grateful to have had the chance to do so in this setting. Special thanks to Jonathan Simon, Rosann Greenspan, and Meg Gentes for making my stay possible and to fellow visiting scholars Sarah Igo, Laverne Jacobs, Yuan Qiao, Marion Vannier, and Rose Cuison Villazor. Special thanks to the University of Arizona's School of Anthropology for a residency that provided a lovely setting as I was finalizing the manuscript.

My home institution, the University of Nevada, Reno, has supported my research in many ways: through leave to conduct fieldwork and to write; funding from the College of Liberal Arts in the form of a Scholarly and Creative Activities Grant, junior faculty summer research support, and travel grants; a Junior Faculty Research Grant and travel support from the Office of the Vice President for Research; and funds from the Gender, Race, and Identity Program. I am fortunate to work with such a collegial group of faculty and faculty associates in both of my academic homes, Anthropology and Women's Studies/Gender, Race, and Identity. There are too many to name individually, so I collectively thank the many colleagues who make our university a wonderful place to be. I am also grateful to work with young people who are passionately committed to social justice and improving the lives of immigrants. I especially appreciate to my students who are engaging with these difficult issues through their research. Special thanks to Maggie Salas Crespo and the group of migrant youth who traveled as part of the "first Dreamers' visit to Mexico City" for their inspiration.

I thank those who read, discussed, and/or provided feedback on sections of the book—informally, in writing groups, at conferences, or as discussants on panels—including Nadine Attewell, Deanna Barenboim, Catherine Besteman, Jennifer Burrell, Jørgen Carling, Leo Chavez, Cati Coe, Susan Bibler Coutin, Sarah Cowie, Shannon Dawdy, Daniel

Enrique Pérez, Caitlin Fouratt, Katherine Fusco, Alyshia Gálvez, Elżbieta M. Goździak, Lauren Heidbrink, Julia Meredith Hess, Joe Heyman, Emily Hobson, Sarah Horton, Jonathan Xavier Inda, Deirdre McKay, Noelle Molé, Meredith Oda, Anna Ochoa O'Leary, Amy Pason, Gautam Premnath, Rachel Reynolds, Mikaela Rogozen-Soltar, Lynn Stephen, Erin Stiles, Rachael Stryker, Heidi Swank, Maria Tapias, George Thomas, S. Trimble, Gaku Tsuda, Brett Van Hoesen, Bill Wagner, and Carolyn White. Thank you to Deborah Achtenberg for engaging conversations about relevant work by philosophers. I am indebted to Jen Hill for her generosity and the time she dedicated to reading and commenting on the full manuscript. Many thanks to Susan Terrio for her mentorship and friendship.

Participation in several workshops provided a chance to think through arguments from disciplinary and interdisciplinary perspectives, including "After the Terror" (Peace Research Institute Oslo, Norway, and University of California, Los Angeles); "Moralities of Migration" (Peace Research Institute Oslo, Norway); "The Concept of Mixed Migration: Reflecting on Today's Migratory Policies, Movements, and Paradigm Shifts" (The Graduate Institute, Geneva, Switzerland); "Migrations and Diaspora" (Tepoztlán Institute, Tepoztlán, Mexico); and a Mellon Workshop titled "Worlds Divided: Interrogating Inequality, Past and Present" (Brown University). Audience questions and discussions at presentations contributed to my thinking about this topic, including those at American Anthropological Association annual meetings; Anthropology of Childhood and Youth Interest Group conferences; Brown University; Centro Sávila in Albuquerque, New Mexico; the UNR College of Liberal Arts Graduate Student Symposium; El Colegio de San Luis in Mexico; Latin American Studies Association congresses; a Reflective Engagement Grant Team meeting at Georgetown University; Society for Applied Anthropology meetings; the School for Advanced Research; Southwestern Anthropological Association meetings; graduate seminars at the Universidad Autónoma de Zacatecas; and the Université de Liège, Belgium.

As always, I am grateful for the love and support of family members, including Robert and Marcia Boehm, Chris Boehm, Carolyn Kelly and Al Rousseau, Kelly and Keenan Jackson, and John, Sherrie, Sierra, and Ila Jackson. I cannot thank enough my partner, Patrick Jackson, and daughter, Ava, for being such willing and adventurous fieldwork companions and for enduring my long work hours, extended travel that took me away from Reno, and far too many weekends at the office. While writing this book, I was discouraged one day to learn that my daughter had read in an elementary school textbook that it is "easy to naturalize as a U.S. citizen" but then heartened when she told me that she knew this to be untrue. In fact, she said, she found such statements "offensive" because she was close to so many people for whom naturalization, or even documented migration, was impossible. Let us hope that those of her generation will continue to question unjust policies and help us find a way out of the chaos that currently envelops deportation and return.

Notes

PROLOGUE

1. Artemio's deportation was first described in Boehm 2011b. Throughout the book, I use pseudonyms for all research participants.
2. See Boehm 2012 for discussion of the effects of migration on family life.

CHAPTER 1

1. Aspects of this chapter, including Mariela's observations, were first published in "'¿Quien Sabe?': Deportation and Temporality among Transnational Mexicans," *Urban Anthropology and Studies of Cultural Systems and World Economic Development* (Boehm 2009).
2. Boehm 2012: 3.
3. See also Yngvesson and Coutin 2006.
4. U.S. Department of Homeland Security 2014: 103.
5. U.S. Department of Homeland Security 2008: 92.
6. Simanski and Sapp 2013.
7. U.S. Department of Homeland Security 2014: 103.
8. U.S. Department of Homeland Security 2008: 95.
9. Ibid.
10. Ibid.
11. Ibid.
12. Kanstroom 2007: 7. See also De Genova 2005.
13. See discussion in Ngai 2004. See also Alanis Enciso 2003; Calavita 1992; De Genova 2005; and Kanstroom 2007 for research about "returns" in U.S.-Mexico history.
14. See Boehm 2012: 150.
15. Stumpf 2006: 379.

16. Stumpf 2006.

17. U.S. Department of Homeland Security 2008: 95.

18. De Genova 2002.

19. Kanstroom 2012: 135.

20. Boehm 2012: 5.

21. Coutin 2007.

22. Ibid.; Peutz 2006; Zilberg 2011.

23. Rhodes 2006: 235.

24. For example, Abrego 2014; Boehm 2012; Coe 2014; Dreby 2010; Foner 2009; Menjívar 2000; Newendorp 2008; Olwig 2007; Parreñas 2005.

25. Some exceptions include Dreby 2015; Golash-Boza 2012; Zayas 2015.

26. Butler 2000; Povinelli 2006; Stevens 1999, 2010. See Bhabha 2014 for a discussion of the right to and respect for family life.

27. See Zilberg 2004: 762.

28. This section draws on Boehm 2009: 354–55.

29. Yngvesson and Coutin 2006: 181.

30. Coe 2016.

31. See Yngvesson and Coutin 2006: 184.

32. Boehm 2008a.

33. Tapias 2006. Also see Holmes 2013 and Horton 2016 for research on how suffering and injustice is embodied by migrants.

34. Bhabha 1998: 612.

35. For example, Chavez 2007, 2008; Coutin 2000, 2005, 2007; De Genova 2002, 2005; Menjívar and Kanstroom 2013; Ngai 2004; Willen 2007.

36. U.S. Internal Revenue Service 2013.

37. Menjívar 2006.

38. Batalova 2008; Krogstad and Passel 2014.

39. Simanski and Sapp 2013.

40. See Boehm 2012: "Postscript: Caught."

41. Biehl 2013: 575.

42. Peutz 2006.

43. De Genova and Peutz 2010.

44. Ong 1999.

45. Kanstroom 2007; Ngai 2004.

46. Chavez 2008; De Genova 2005; Rosas 2012.

47. Bhabha 1998; Coutin 2010; De Genova 2010; Dowling and Inda 2013; Peutz 2007; Zilberg 2011.

48. Andersson 2014; Coutin 2007; De Genova and Peutz 2010; Heyman 1995, 1999; Inda 2006; Peutz 2006, 2007.

49. For example, Potter, Conway, and Phillips 2005; Tsuda 2009.

50. For example, Long and Oxfeld 2004; Markowitz and Stefansson 2004.

51. Coutin 2000: 27.

52. Peutz 2006: 223.

53. Derrida 1994: 10.

54. Peutz 2006: 231.

CHAPTER 2

1. For example, De Genova 2002; Stumpf 2006.

2. Derrida 1994: 103.

3. For example, Derrida and Dufourmantelle 2000: 15.

4. Derrida and Dufourmantelle 2000; Jabès 1988; Levinas 1991.

5. Some of David's conversations with me (using the pseudonym José) are also recounted in Boehm 2009.

6. NV Ref. Stat. 396.930 2013.

7. Krogstad and Passel 2014.

8. De Genova 2002: 422.

9. Ibid., 439.

10. U.S. Immigration and Customs Enforcement 2010.

11. This meeting and other sections of this chapter were first described in Boehm 2009.

12. Foucault 1977: 73.

13. Coutin 2010.

14. Ibid., 353.

15. Boehm 2012: 149.

16. I described Carlos (using the pseudonym Pedro) in Boehm 2009.

17. Kanstroom 2012: 135.

18. Rabin 2011.

19. Ibid.

20. Rabin 2009.

CHAPTER 3

1. Sections of this chapter first appeared in "US-Mexico Mixed Migration in an Age of Deportation: An Inquiry into the Transnational Circulation of Violence," *Refugee Survey Quarterly* (Boehm 2011b).

2. For work on insecurity and uncertainty in other settings, see, for example, Burrell 2013; Goldstein 2010, 2012; James 2010; Moodie 2010; Niehaus 2013.

3. Boehm 2011b.

4. Green 1999.

5. Scheper-Hughes and Bourgois 2004: 2.

6. Ibid., 1, 5.

7. Ibid., 13–14.

8. Scheper-Hughes and Bourgois 2004.

9. Galtung 1969.

10. Bourdieu and Wacquant 2004.

11. Galtung 1969: 170. See also Bourgois 2004; Farmer 2004.

12. Galtung 1990.

13. Coutin 2010: 353.

14. Farmer 2004: 308.

15. Farmer 1997.

16. Farmer 2004: 307.

17. Ibid.

18. Das 2007: 9.

19. *Los Angeles Times* n.d.

20. Cave 2012.

21. *Le Monde* 2012.

22. *Informador* 2013.

23. See also Muehlmann 2013.

24. *New York Times* 2010.

25. This experience was first described using different pseudonyms in Boehm 2011b: 13.

26. Dillon 2009.

27. Ibid.

28. Knight 2010.

29. Stillman 2015.

30. De León 2015.

31. Terrio 2015.

32. Bernstein 2009.

33. Inda 2006: 32.

34. Ibid., 108, 175, 109.

35. De Genova and Peutz 2010; Dowling and Inda 2013; Inda 2006.

36. Bourgois 1996: 114.

37. See also Peutz 2007.

38. Foucault 1997: 200, 201.

39. Ibid., 200.

40. Zigon 2008: 79.

41. Boehm 2008a.

42. Dowling and Inda 2013.

43. Nyers 2003: 1072–73.

44. Goldstein 2012: 7, 3.

45. Heyman 1999.

46. Boehm 2012.

47. Galtung 1969.

CHAPTER 4

1. Butler and Athanasiou 2013: 2. Also see Kasmir and Carbonella 2008 for a discussion of dispossession.

2. Sassen 2014.

3. Butler and Athanasiou 2013: 5.

4. Ibid., 20, 2. Also see Muehlebach 2013 for anthropological work on precarity.

5. Dreby 2010.

6. Coe 2014.

7. See Gupta and Ferguson 1997:50.

8. De Genova 2010: 33.

9. Boehm 2008b, 2012.

10. Boehm 2012: 96.

11. Golash-Boza and Hondagneu-Sotelo 2013: 281.

12. See discussion in Boehm et al. 2011: 4.

13. For example, Donato et al. 2006; Hondagneu-Sotelo 1994, 2003; Mahler and Pessar 2001; Pessar and Mahler 2003.

14. Boehm 2012: 41.

15. Mahler and Pessar 2001.

16. Butler 2004b.

17. Ibid., 103.

18. Boehm 2012: 57.

19. Boehm 2012.

20. Ibid., 62–63.

21. Boehm 2011a: 168.

22. Coutin 2000.

23. Boehm 2011a: 168.

CHAPTER 5

1. Capps et al. 2007.

2. Wessler 2011.

3. Passel and Cohn 2009.

4. See also Coutin 2010; Zayas 2015.

5. Zilberg 2004: 761.

6. Bhabha 1999: xii.

7. Naficy 1999: 4.

8. Ibid., 9. See also Hess 2009.

9. Naficy 1999: 9.

10. Ibid.

11. Coutin 2010.

12. See Boehm 2011a.

13. Tsing 1993.

14. Kanstroom 2012: 135.

15. Plascencia 2009: 410.

16. Bhabha 1999: xii.

17. Chavez 2008.

18. See Ngai 2004.

19. Rabin 2011.

20. Boehm 2011a: 162.

21. Menjívar and Abrego 2012.

22. Abrego 2014: 91.

23. Menjívar 2006.

24. Ibid.; Abrego 2014.

25. Abrego 2014; Dreby 2015.

26. Gonzales 2015.

27. See Gonzales and Chavez 2012.

28. Boehm 2011a; 2012: 133–138. Also see discussion in Ngai 2004.

29. Schein 1997: 477.

30. Hess 2009: 212.

31. Appiah 2006: xxi.

32. Ibid., xv.

33. Zilberg 2004: 762.
34. Douglas 1966.
35. Pollock et al. 2002: 5.
36. See Robbins 1992.
37. Ong 1999.
38. Clifford 1992: 108.
39. Schein 1997: 483.
40. Robbins 1992: 176.
41. See Ong 1999.
42. Kelsky 2001: 13.
43. Pollock et al. 2002: 6.
44. For a discussion of some of the educational challenges for transnational children, see Hamann and Zúñiga 2011.
45. Bhabha 1999: xii.
46. Coutin 2010: 361; original emphasis.
47. Ibid., 355.
48. Bhabha 1994; Schuck 1998.
49. Malkki 1995: 1–2.
50. Maira 2009.
51. Ibid., 35.
52. Malkki 1995: 19.
53. Bhabha 1994.
54. Coutin 2005: 196.
55. See discussion in Boehm 2012: 112–15; Boehm et al. 2011: 4.

CHAPTER 6

1. Agamben 2005.
2. Nussbaum 2006.
3. The discussion of transnationalism, here and in other sections of the chapter, draw on Boehm 2009.
4. Rouse 1992: 46. See discussion in Boehm 2012: 145.
5. For example, Boehm 2012; Kearney 1998, 2004; Rouse 1991, 1992; Smith 2006; Stephen 2007.
6. Coutin 2007; Peutz 2006; Zilberg 2011.
7. See discussion in Aretxaga 2003.
8. Aretxaga 2003: 393.
9. For example, Appadurai 2006; Aretxaga 2003; Kearney 1998; Ong 1999; Rosas 2012; Tsing 2005. See related discussion in Boehm 2012: 55–56.
10. Tsing 2005.
11. Appadurai 2006: x.
12. Fassin 2011: 221. See also De Genova and Peutz 2010; Dowling and Inda 2013; Heyman 1999; Rosas 2012.
13. See Boehm 2009.
14. Harvey 1989: 213.
15. Ibid., 214.
16. Ibid., 202.

17. Gingrich, Ochs, and Swedlund 2002: S3.
18. Das 2007: 16. See also Fassin 2011.
19. Butler 2004b: 80.
20. Kondo 1990.
21. Butler 2004b: 217.
22. Agamben 1999: 177.
23. Ibid., 181, 177.
24. Ibid., 180.
25. Butler 2004b: 91.
26. Peutz 2010: 391.
27. Ibid.
28. Butler 2004b: 219.
29. Boehm 2011a.
30. See Coutin 2007: 116.
31. Kanstroom 2012.
32. Passel and Cohn 2014.
33. Also described in Boehm 2009.
34. Coutin 2007: 44.
35. De León 2015.
36. Passel and Cohn 2012.
37. Coutin 2005: 196.

EPILOGUE

1. See Boehm 2012.
2. Boehm 2012: 149.
3. Coutin 2007: 44.
4. For work on "abandonment" and "social death," see, for example, Alexander 2010; Biehl 2005; Cacho 2012; Coutin 2007; Patterson 1985; Povinelli 2011.
5. Butler 2004a.
6. Ibid., 20; original emphasis.
7. Derrida 2001.
8. Butler 2004a.

Bibliography

Abrego, Leisy J. 2014. *Sacrificing Families: Navigating Laws, Labor, and Love across Borders*. Stanford, CA: Stanford University Press.

Agamben, Giorgio. 1999. *Potentialities*. Stanford, CA: Stanford University Press.

———. 2005. *State of Exception*. Translated by Kevin Attell. Chicago: University of Chicago Press.

Alanis Enciso, Fernando Saúl. 2003. "'No cuenten conmigo': El gobierno de México y la repatriación de mexicanos de Estados Unidos 1910–1928." *Mexican Studies/Estudios Mexicanos* 19 (2): 401–31.

Alexander, Michelle. 2010. *The New Jim Crow: Mass Incarceration in the Age of Colorblindness*. New York: New Press.

Andersson, Ruben. 2014. *Illegality, Inc: Migration and the Business of Bordering Europe*. Berkeley: University of California Press.

Appadurai, Arjun. 2006. *Fear of Small Numbers: An Essay on the Geography of Anger*. Durham, NC: Duke University Press.

Appiah, Kwame Anthony. 2006. *Cosmopolitanism: Ethics in a World of Strangers*. New York: W. W. Norton.

Aretxaga, Begoña. 2003. "Maddening States." *Annual Review of Anthropology* 32: 393–410.

Batalova, Jeanne. 2008. "Mexican Immigrants in the United States." A Report by the Migration Policy Institute, April. www.migrationinformation.org.

Bernstein, Nina. 2009. "Officials Say Detainee Deaths Were Missed." *New York Times*, January 17.

Bhabha, Homi K. 1994. *The Location of Culture*. London: Routledge.

———. 1999. "Preface: Arrivals and Departures." In *Home, Exile, Homeland: Film, Media, and the Politics of Place*, edited by Hamid Naficy, vii–xii. New York: Routledge.

Bhabha, Jacqueline. 1998. "'Get Back to Where You Once Belonged': Identity, Citizenship, and Exclusion in Europe." *Human Rights Quarterly* 20: 592–727.

———. 2014. *Child Migration and Human Rights in a Global Age.* Princeton, NJ: Princeton University Press.

Biehl, João. 2005. *Vita: Life in a Zone of Social Abandonment.* Berkeley: University of California Press.

———. 2013. "Ethnography in the Way of Theory." *Cultural Anthropology* 28 (4): 573–97.

Boehm, Deborah A. 2008a. "'For My Children': Constructing Family and Navigating the State in the U.S.-Mexico Transnation." *Anthropological Quarterly* 81 (4): 777–802.

———. 2008b. "'Now I Am a Man and a Woman!': Gendered Moves and Migrations in a Transnational Mexican Community." *Latin American Perspectives* 35 (1): 16–30.

———. 2009. "'¿Quien Sabe?': Deportation and Temporality among Transnational Mexicans." *Urban Anthropology and Studies of Cultural Systems and World Economic Development* 38 (2–4): 345–74.

———. 2011a. "Here/Not Here: Contingent Citizenship and Transnational Mexican Children." In *Everyday Ruptures: Children and Migration in Global Perspective,* edited by Cati Coe, Rachel Reynolds, Deborah A. Boehm, Julia Meredith Hess, and Heather Rae-Espinoza, 161–73. Nashville, TN: Vanderbilt University Press.

———. 2011b. "US-Mexico Mixed Migration in an Age of Deportation: An Inquiry into the Transnational Circulation of Violence." *Refugee Survey Quarterly* 30 (1): 1–21.

———. 2012. *Intimate Migrations: Gender, Family, and Illegality among Transnational Mexicans.* New York: New York University Press.

Boehm, Deborah A., Julia Meredith Hess, Cati Coe, Heather Rae-Espinoza, and Rachel R. Reynolds. 2011. "Introduction: Children, Youth, and the Everyday Ruptures of Migration." In *Everyday Ruptures: Children and Migration in Global Perspective,* edited by Cati Coe, Rachel Reynolds, Deborah A. Boehm, Julia Meredith Hess, and Heather Rae-Espinoza, 1–19. Nashville, TN: Vanderbilt University Press.

Bourdieu, Pierre, and Loïc Wacquant. 2004. "Symbolic Violence." In *Violence in War and Peace: An Anthology,* edited by Nancy Scheper-Hughes and Philippe Bourgois, 272–74. Oxford: Blackwell.

Bourgois, Philippe. 1996. *In Search of Respect: Selling Crack in El Barrio.* Cambridge: Cambridge University Press.

———. 2004. "U.S. Inner-City Apartheid: The Contours of Structural and Interpersonal Violence." In *Violence in War and Peace: An Anthology,* edited by Nancy Scheper-Hughes and Philippe Bourgois, 301–7. Oxford: Blackwell.

Burrell, Jennifer L. 2013. *Maya after War: Conflict, Power, and Politics in Guatemala.* Austin: University of Texas Press.

Butler, Judith. 2000. *Antigone's Claim: Kinship between Life and Death.* New York: Columbia University Press.

———. 2004a. *Precarious Life: The Powers of Mourning and Violence.* London: Verso.

———. 2004b. *Undoing Gender.* New York: Routledge.

Butler, Judith, and Athena Athanasiou. 2013. *Dispossession: The Performative in the Political.* Cambridge: Polity Press.

Cacho, Lisa Marie. 2012. *Social Death: Racialized Righteousness and the Criminalization of the Unprotected.* New York: New York University Press.

Calavita, Kitty. 1992. *Inside the State: The Bracero Program, Immigration, and the I.N.S.* New York: Routledge.

Capps, Randy, Rose Maria Castañeda, Ajay Chaudry, and Robert Santos. 2007. "Paying the Price: The Impact of Immigration Raids on America's Children." A Report by the Urban Institute. Washington, DC: National Council of La Raza. www.urban.org/research/publication/paying-price-impact-immigration-raids-americas-children

Cave, Damien. 2012. "Mexico Updates Death Toll in Drug War to 47,515, but Critics Dispute the Data." *New York Times,* January 11.

Chavez, Leo R. 2007. "The Condition of Illegality." *International Migration* 45 (3): 192–95.

———. 2008. *The Latino Threat: Constructing Immigrants, Citizens, and the Nation.* Stanford, CA: Stanford University Press.

Clifford, James. 1992. "Traveling Cultures." In *Cultural Studies,* edited by Lawrence Grossberg, Cary Nelson, and Paula A. Treichler, 96–112. New York: Routledge.

Coe, Cati. 2014. *The Scattered Family: Parenting, African Migrants, and Global Inequality.* Chicago: University of Chicago Press.

———. 2016. "Orchestrating Care in Time: Ghanaian Migrant Women, Family and Reciprocity." *American Anthropologist.* doi:10.1111/aman.12446.

Coutin, Susan Bibler. 2000. *Legalizing Moves: Salvadoran Immigrants' Struggle for U.S. Residency.* Ann Arbor: University of Michigan Press.

———. 2005. "Being En Route." *American Anthropologist* 107 (2): 195–206.

———. 2007. *Nations of Emigrants: Shifting Boundaries of Citizenship in El Salvador and the United States.* Ithaca, NY: Cornell University Press.

———. 2010. "Exiled by Law: Deportation and the Inviability of Life." In *The Deportation Regime: Sovereignty, Space, and the Freedom of Movement,* edited by Nicholas De Genova and Nathalie Peutz, 351–70. Durham, NC: Duke University Press.

Das, Veena. 2007. *Life and Words: Violence and the Descent into the Ordinary.* Berkeley: University of California Press.

De Genova, Nicholas. 2002. "Migrant 'Illegality' and Deportability in Everyday Life." *Annual Review of Anthropology* 31: 419–47.

———. 2005. *Working the Boundaries: Race, Space, and "Illegality" in Mexican Chicago.* Durham, NC: Duke University Press.

———. 2010. "The Deportation Regime: Sovereignty, Space, and the Freedom of Movement." In *The Deportation Regime: Sovereignty, Space, and the Freedom of Movement,* edited by Nicholas De Genova and Nathalie Peutz, 33–65. Durham, NC: Duke University Press.

De Genova, Nicholas, and Nathalie Peutz, eds. 2010. *The Deportation Regime: Sovereignty, Space, and the Freedom of Movement.* Durham, NC: Duke University Press.

De León, Jason. 2015. *The Land of Open Graves: Living and Dying on the Migrant Trail*. Berkeley: University of California Press.

Derrida, Jacques. 1994. *Specters of Marx: The State of the Debt, the Work of Mourning and the New International*. New York: Routledge Classics.

———. 2001. *The Work of Mourning*. Edited by Pascale-Anne Brault and Michael Naas. Chicago: University of Chicago Press.

Derrida, Jacques, and Anne Dufourmantelle. 2000. *Of Hospitality: Anne Dufourmantelle Invites Jacques Derrida to Respond*. Stanford, CA: Stanford University Press.

Dillon, Sam. 2009. "Kidnappings in Mexico Send Shivers across Border." *New York Times,* January 4.

Donato, Katharine M., Donna Gabaccia, Jennifer Holdaway, Martin Manalansan IV, and Patricia R. Pessar. 2006. "A Glass Half Full? Gender in Migration Studies." *International Migration Review* 40 (1): 3–26.

Douglas, Mary. 1966. *Purity and Danger: An Analysis of Concepts of Pollution and Taboo*. London: Routledge.

Dowling, Julie A., and Jonathan Xavier Inda, eds. 2013. *Governing Immigration through Crime: A Reader*. Stanford, CA: Stanford University Press.

Dreby, Joanna. 2010. *Divided by Borders: Mexican Migrants and Their Children*. Berkeley: University of California Press.

———. 2015. *Everyday Illegal: When Policies Undermine Immigrant Families*. Berkeley: University of California Press.

Farmer, Paul. 1997. *Pathologies of Power: Health, Human Rights, and the New War on the Poor*. Berkeley: University of California Press.

———. 2004. "An Anthropology of Structural Violence." *Current Anthropology* 45 (3): 305–25.

Fassin, Didier. 2011. "Policing Borders, Producing Boundaries: The Governmentality of Immigration in Dark Times." *Annual Review of Anthropology* 40: 213–26.

Foner, Nancy, ed. 2009. *Across Generations: Immigrant Families in America*. New York: New York University Press.

Foucault, Michel. 1977. *Discipline and Punish: The Birth of the Prison*. New York: Pantheon Books.

Galtung, Johan. 1969. "Violence, Peace, and Peace Research." *Journal of Peace Research* 6 (3): 167–91.

———. 1990. "Cultural Violence." *Journal of Peace Research* 27 (3): 291–305.

Gingrich, Andre, Elinor Ochs, and Alan Swedlund. 2002. "Repertoires of Timekeeping in Anthropology." *Current Anthropology* 43: S3–S4.

Golash-Boza, Tanya Maria. 2012. *Immigration Nation: Raids, Detentions, and Deportations in Post-9/11 America*. Boulder, CO: Paradigm.

Golash-Boza, Tanya Maria, and Pierrette Hondagneu-Sotelo. 2013. "Latino Immigrant Men and the Deportation Crisis: A Gendered Racial Removal Program." *Latino Studies* 11: 271–92.

Goldstein, Daniel M. 2010. "Toward a Critical Anthropology of Security." *Current Anthropology* 51 (4): 487–517.

———. 2012. *Outlawed: Between Security and Rights in a Bolivian City*. Durham, NC: Duke University Press.

Gonzales, Roberto G. 2015. *Lives in Limbo: Undocumented and Coming of Age in America*. Berkeley: University of California Press.

Gonzales, Roberto G., and Leo R. Chavez. 2012. "'Awakening to a Nightmare': Abjectivity and Illegality in the Lives of Undocumented 1.5 Generation Latino Immigrants in the United States." *Current Anthropology* 53 (3): 268–69.

Green, Linda. 1999. *Fear as a Way of Life: Mayan Widows in Rural Guatemala*. New York: Columbia University Press.

Gupta, Akhil and James Ferguson. 1997. "Beyond 'Culture': Space, Identity, and the Politics of Difference." In *Culture, Power, Place: Explorations in Critical Anthropology*, edited by Akhil Gupta and James Ferguson, 33–51. Durham, NC: Duke University Press.

Hamann, Edmund T., and Victor Zúñiga. 2011. "Schooling and the Everyday Ruptures Transnational Children Encounter in the United States and Mexico." In *Everyday Ruptures: Children and Migration in Global Perspective*, edited by Cati Coe, Rachel Reynolds, Deborah A. Boehm, Julia Meredith Hess, and Heather Rae-Espinoza, 141–60. Nashville, TN: Vanderbilt University Press.

Harvey, David. 1989. *The Condition of Postmodernity: An Enquiry into the Origins of Cultural Change*. Oxford: Blackwell.

Hess, Julia Meredith. 2009. *Immigrant Ambassadors: Citizenship and Belonging in the Tibetan Diaspora*. Stanford, CA: Stanford University Press.

Heyman, Josiah McC. 1995. "Putting Power into the Anthropology of Bureaucracy: The Immigration and Naturalization Service at the Mexico–United States Border." *Current Anthropology* 36 (2): 261–87.

———. 1999. *States and Illegal Practices*. Oxford: Berg.

Holmes, Seth M. 2013. *Fresh Fruit, Broken Bodies: Migrant Farmworkers in the United States*. Berkeley: University of California Press.

Hondagneu-Sotelo, Pierrette. 1994. *Gendered Transitions: Mexican Experiences of Immigration*. Berkeley: University of California Press.

———, ed. 2003. *Gender and U.S. Immigration: Contemporary Trends*. Berkeley: University of California Press.

Horton, Sarah. 2016. *They Leave Their Kidneys in the Fields: Injury, Illness, and Illegality among U.S. Farmworkers*. Berkeley: University of California Press.

Inda, Jonathan Xavier. 2006. *Targeting Immigrants: Government, Technology, and Ethics*. Malden, MA: Wiley-Blackwell.

Informador. 2013. "Con Peña Nieto, 52 muertos diarios." www.informador .com.mx/mexico/2013/482393/6/con-pena-nieto-52-muertos-diarios.htm.

Jabès, Edmond. 1988. *If There Were Anywhere but Desert: The Selected Poems of Edmond Jabès*. Barrytown, NY: Station Hill Press.

James, Erica Caple. 2010. *Democratic Insecurities: Violence, Trauma, and Intervention in Haiti*. Berkeley: University of California Press.

Kanstroom, Daniel. 2007. *Deportation Nation: Outsiders in American History*. Cambridge, MA: Harvard University Press.

———. 2012. *Aftermath: Deportation Law and the New American Diaspora*. Oxford: Oxford University Press.

Kasmir, Sharryn, and August Carbonella. 2008. "Dispossession and the Anthropology of Labor." *Critique of Anthropology* 28 (1): 5–25.

Kearney, Michael. 1998. "Transnationalism in California and Mexico at the End of Empire." In *Border Identities: Nation and State at International Frontiers,* edited by Thomas M. Wilson and Hastings Donnan, 117–41. Cambridge: Cambridge University Press.

———. 2004. *Changing Fields of Anthropology: From Local to Global.* Lanham, MD: Rowman and Littlefield.

Kelsky, Karen. 2001. *Women on the Verge: Japanese Women, Western Dreams.* Durham, NC: Duke University Press.

Knight, Meribah. 2010. "Families Fear Phone Call from Mexico's Cartels." *New York Times,* July 31.

Kondo, Dorinne K. 1990. *Crafting Selves: Power, Gender, and Discourses of Identity in a Japanese Workplace.* Chicago: University of Chicago Press.

Krogstad, Jens Manuel, and Jeffrey S. Passel. 2014. "5 Facts about Illegal Immigration in the U.S." Pew Research Center. www.pewresearch.org/fact-tank /2015/11/19/5-facts-about-illegal-immigration-in-the-u-s/.

Levinas, Emmanuel. 1991. *Totality and Infinity.* Dordrecht: Kluwer Academic.

Long, Lynellyn D., and Ellen Oxfeld, eds. 2004. *Coming Home? Refugees, Migrants, and Those Who Stayed Behind.* Philadelphia: University of Pennsylvania Press.

Los Angeles Times. n.d. "Mexico under Siege." www.latimes.com/world /drug-war/.

Mahler, Sarah J., and Patricia R. Pessar. 2001. "Gendered Geographies of Power: Analyzing Gender across Transnational Spaces." *Identities* 7 (4): 441–59.

Maira, Sunaina Marr. 2009. *Missing: Youth, Citizenship, and Empire after 9/11.* Durham, NC: Duke University Press.

Malkki, Liisa H. 1995. *Purity and Exile: Violence, Memory, and National Cosmology among Hutu Refugees in Tanzania.* Chicago: University of Chicago Press.

Markowitz, Fran, and Anders H. Stefansson, eds. 2004. *Homecomings: Unsettling Paths of Return.* New York: Lexington Books.

Menjívar, Cecilia. 2000. *Fragmented Ties: Salvadoran Immigrant Ties in America.* Berkeley: University of California Press.

———. 2006. "Liminal Legality: Salvadoran and Guatemalan Immigrants' Lives in the United States." *American Journal of Sociology* 111 (4): 999–1037.

Menjívar, Cecilia, and Leisy J. Abrego. 2012. "Legal Violence: Immigration Law and the Lives of Central American Immigrants." *American Journal of Sociology* 117 (5): 1380–1421.

Menjívar, Cecilia, and Daniel Kanstroom, eds. 2013. *Constructing Immigrant "Illegality": Critiques, Experiences, and Responses.* Cambridge: Cambridge University Press.

Le Monde. 2012. "Mexique, la spirale de la barbarie." www.lemonde.fr/idees /article/2012/08/23/mexique-la-spirale-de-la-barbarie_1749042_3232.html.

Moodie, Ellen. 2010. *El Salvador in the Aftermath of Peace: Crime, Uncertainty, and the Transition to Democracy.* Philadelphia: University of Pennsylvania Press.

Muehlebach, Andrea. 2013. "On Precariousness and the Ethical Imagination: The Year 2012 in Sociocultural Anthropology." *American Anthropologist* 115 (2): 297–311.

Muehlmann, Shaylih. 2013. *When I Wear My Alligator Boots: Narco-Culture in the U.S.-Mexico Borderlands*. Berkeley: University of California Press.

Naficy, Hamid. 1999. "Introduction—Framing Exile: From Homeland to Homepage." In *Home, Exile, Homeland: Film, Media, and the Politics of Place*, edited by Hamid Naficy, 1–16. New York: Routledge.

Newendorp, Nicole. 2008. *Uneasy Reunions: Immigration, Citizenship, and Family Life in Post-1997 Hong Kong*. Stanford, CA: Stanford University Press.

New York Times. 2010. "Drug War Refugees Seek Asylum at the Texas Border." Slide show accompanying article, April 17. www.nytimes.com /slideshow/2010/04/17/us/0418EXODUS_index.html?_r=0.

Ngai, Mae M. 2004. *Impossible Subjects: Illegal Aliens and the Making of Modern America*. Princeton, NJ: Princeton University Press.

Niehaus, Isak. 2013. "Confronting Uncertainty: Anthropology and Zones of the Extraordinary." *American Ethnologist* 40 (4): 651–60.

Nussbaum, Martha C. 2006. *Hiding from Humanity: Disgust, Shame, and the Law*. Princeton, NJ: Princeton University Press.

Nyers, Peter. 2003. "Abject Cosmopolitanism: The Politics of Protection in the Anti-Deportation Movement." *Third World Quarterly* 24 (6): 1069–93.

Olwig, Karen. 2007. *Caribbean Journeys: An Ethnography of Migration and Home in Three Family Networks*. Durham, NC: Duke University Press.

Ong, Aihwa. 1999. *Flexible Citizenship: The Cultural Logics of Transnationality*. Durham, NC: Duke University Press.

Parreñas, Rhacel Salazar. 2005. *Children of Global Migration: Transnational Families and Gendered Woes*. Stanford, CA: Stanford University Press.

Passel, Jeffrey S., and D'Vera Cohn. 2009. "A Portrait of Unauthorized Immigrants in the United States." Pew Research Center. www.pewhispanic.org /2009/04/14/a-portrait-of-unauthorized-immigrants-in-the-united-states/.

———. 2012. "Unauthorized Immigrants: 11.1 Million in 2011." Pew Research Center. www.pewhispanic.org/2012/12/06/unauthorized-immigrants-11-1 -million-in-2011/.

———. 2014. "Unauthorized Immigrant Totals Rise in 7 States, Fall in 14." Pew Research Center. www.pewhispanic.org/2014/11/18/unauthorized- immigrant-totals-rise-in-7-states-fall-in-14/.

Patterson, Orlando. 1985. *Slavery and Social Death: A Comparative Study*. Cambridge, MA: Harvard University Press.

Pessar, Patricia R., and Sarah J. Mahler. 2003. "Transnational Migration: Bringing Gender In." *International Migration Review* 37 (3): 812–46.

Peutz, Nathalie. 2006. "Embarking on an Anthropology of Removal." *Current Anthropology* 47 (2): 217–31.

———. 2007. "Out-laws: Deportees, Desire, and 'The Law.'" *International Migration* 45 (3): 182–91.

———. 2010. "'Criminal Alien' Deportees in Somaliland: An Ethnography of Removal." In *The Deportation Regime: Sovereignty, Space, and the Freedom of Movement,* edited by Nicholas De Genova and Nathalie Peutz, 371–409. Durham, NC: Duke University Press.

Plascencia, Luis F. B. 2009. "The 'Undocumented' Mexican Migrant Question: Re-Examining the Framing of Law and Illegalization in the United States." *Urban Anthropology and Studies of Cultural Systems and World Economic Development* 38 (2–4): 375–434.

Pollock, Sheldon, Homi K. Bhabha, Carol A. Breckenridge, and Dipesh Chakrabarty. 2002. "Cosmopolitanisms." In *Cosmopolitanism,* edited by Carol A. Breckenridge, Sheldon Pollock, Homi K. Bhabha and Dipesh Chakrabarty, 1–14. Durham, NC: Duke University Press.

Potter, Robert, Dennis Conway, and Joan Phillips, eds. 2005. *The Experience of Return Migration: Caribbean Perspectives.* Burlington, VT: Ashgate.

Povinelli, Elizabeth A. 2006. *The Empire of Love: Toward a Theory of Intimacy, Genealogy, and Carnality.* Durham, NC: Duke University Press.

———. 2011. *Economies of Abandonment: Social Belonging and Endurance in Late Liberalism.* Durham, NC: Duke University Press.

Rabin, Nina. 2009. "Unseen Prisoners: A Report on Women in Immigration Detention Facilities in Arizona." Southwest Institute for Research on Women, College of Social and Behavioral Sciences and Bacon Immigration Law and Policy Program, James E. Rogers College of Law at the University of Arizona. https://law2.arizona.edu/depts/bacon_program/pdf/Unseen_Prisoners.pdf.

———. 2011. "Disappearing Parents: Immigration Enforcement and the Child Welfare System." Southwest Institute for Research on Women, College of Social and Behavioral Sciences and Bacon Immigration Law and Policy Program, James E. Rogers College of Law at the University of Arizona. https://law2.arizona.edu/depts/bacon_program/pdf/disappearing_parents_report_final.pdf.

Rhodes, Lorna A. 2006. "Comments—Embarking on an Anthropology of Removal by Nathalie Peutz." *Current Anthropology* 47 (2): 235–37.

Robbins, Bruce. 1992. "Comparative Cosmopolitanism." *Social Text* 31–32: 169–86.

Rosas, Gilberto. 2012. *Barrio Libre: Criminalizing States and Delinquent Refusals of the New Frontier.* Durham, NC: Duke University Press.

Rouse, Roger. 1991. "Mexican Migration and the Social Space of Postmodernism." *Diaspora* 1 (1): 8–23.

———. 1992. "Making Sense of Settlement: Class Transformation, Cultural Struggle, and Transnationalism among Mexican Migrants in the United States." In *Towards a Transnational Perspective on Migration,* edited by Nina Glick Schiller, Linda Basch, and Cristina Blanc-Szanton, 25–52. New York: New York Academy of Sciences.

Sassen, Saskia. 2014. *Expulsions: Brutality and Complexity in the Global Economy.* Cambridge, MA: Harvard University Press.

Schein, Louisa. 1997. "The Consumption of Color and the Politics of White Skin in Post-Mao China." In *The Gender/Sexuality Reader: Culture, History, Political Economy,* edited by Roger N. Lancaster and Micaela di Leonardo, 473–86. New York: Routledge.

Scheper-Hughes, Nancy, and Philippe Bourgois. 2004. "Introduction: Making Sense of Violence." In *Violence in War and Peace: An Anthology,* edited by Nancy Scheper-Hughes and Philippe Bourgois, 1–31. Oxford: Blackwell.

Schuck, Peter H. 1998. *Citizens, Strangers, and In-Betweens.* Boulder, CO: Westview Press.

Simanski, John F., and Lesley M. Sapp. 2013. "Immigration Enforcement Actions: 2012." Office of Immigration Statistics, U.S. Department of Homeland Security. www.dhs.gov/sites/default/files/publications/ois_enforcement _ar_2012_1.pdf.

Smith, Robert C. 2006. *Mexican New York: Transnational Lives of New Immigrants.* Berkeley: University of California Press.

Stephen, Lynn. 2007. *Transborder Lives: Indigenous Oaxacans in Mexico, California, and Oregon.* Durham, NC: Duke University Press.

Stevens, Jacqueline. 1999. *Reproducing the State.* Princeton, NJ: Princeton University Press.

———. 2010. *States without Nations: Citizenship for Mortals.* New York: Columbia University Press.

Stillman, Sarah. 2015. "Where Are the Children?" *New Yorker,* April 27.

Stumpf, Juliet. 2006. "The Crimmigration Crisis: Immigrants, Crime, and Sovereign Power." *American University Law Review* 56: 367–419.

Tapias, Maria. 2006. "Emotions and the Intergenerational Embodiment of Social Suffering in Rural Bolivia." *Medical Anthropology Quarterly* 20 (3): 399–415.

Terrio, Susan. 2015. *Whose Child Am I? Unaccompanied, Undocumented Children in the U.S.* Berkeley: University of California Press.

Tsing, Anna Lowenhaupt. 1993. *In the Realm of the Diamond Queen: Marginality in an Out-of-the-Way Place.* Princeton, NJ: Princeton University Press.

———. 2005. *Friction: An Ethnography of Global Connection.* Princeton, NJ: Princeton University Press.

Tsuda, Takeyuki (Gaku), ed. 2009. *Diasporic Homecomings: Ethnic Return Migrants in Comparative Perspective.* Stanford, CA: Stanford University Press.

U.S. Department of Homeland Security. 2008. "Yearbook of Immigration Statistics: 2007." www.dhs.gov/xlibrary/assets/statistics/yearbook/2007/ois_2007 _yearbook.pdf.

———. 2014. "Yearbook of Immigration Statistics: 2013." www.dhs.gov/sites/ default/files/publications/ois_yb_2013_0.pdf.

U.S. Immigration and Customs Enforcement. 2010. News Release. [No longer available online.]

U.S. Internal Revenue Service. 2013. "U.S. Tax Guide for Aliens." www.irs.gov/ pub/irs-pdf/p519.pdf.

Wessler, Seth Freed. 2011. "Shattered Families: The Perilous Intersection of Immigration Enforcement and the Child Welfare System." Race Forward (formerly Applied Research Center). www.raceforward.org/research/reports/ shattered-families.

Willen, Sarah. 2007. "Toward a Critical Phenomenology of 'Illegality': State Power, Criminalization, and Embodied Experience among Undocumented Migrant Workers in Tel Aviv, Israel." *International Migration* 45 (3): 8–38.

Yngvesson, Barbara, and Susan Bibler Coutin. 2006. "Backed by Papers: Undoing Persons, Histories, and Return." *American Ethnologist* 33 (2): 177–90.

Zayas, Luis H. 2015. *Forgotten Citizens: Deportation, Children, and the Making of American Exiles and Orphans.* Oxford: Oxford University Press.

Zigon, Jarrett. 2008. *Morality: An Anthropological Perspective.* Oxford: Berg.

Zilberg, Elana. 2004. "Fools Banished from the Kingdom: Remapping Geographies of Gang Violence between the Americas (Los Angeles and San Salvador)." *American Quarterly* 56 (3): 759–79.

———. 2011. *Space of Detention: The Making of a Transnational Gang Crisis between Los Angeles and San Salvador.* Durham, NC: Duke University Press.

Index

CPSIA information can be obtained
at www.ICGtesting.com
Printed in the USA
LVHW03s0007200818
587484LV00001B/121/P